THE AGONY OF WINNING

THE AGONY OF WINNING

Seven Strategies for Winning Bigger with Greater Freedom, Spirit, and Integrity

Strategy One: Agony of Winning Triangle: The Who, What, and Why of Athletics

Strategy Two: Competing with Purpose and Passion

Strategy Three: Maintaining a Balance of Intrinsic and Extrinsic Goals

Strategy Four: The Agony of Winning Code of Ethics: Setting a Tone for Integrity, Respect, and Civility

Strategy Five: Overcoming the Pressure to Succeed

Strategy Six: Establishing a System of Core Values

Strategy Seven: Process-Based Athletics, Letting Go of the Outcome.

What Coaches and Parents are Saying About
THE AGONY OF WINNING

In *The Agony of Winning*, Kevin Touhey illustrates how attitudes, optimism, and life-skill development translate into success for coaches, players, and parents while not requiring one to sacrifice winning. As the head football coach of a program that transformed from one win in 2006 to nine wins and our first bowl game in thirty years in 2009, I can share with you that it was our unwavering commitment to executing a process both on and off the field where core values and life-skill development served as the foundation that resulted in this cultural transformation. The Temple Football Owls are a testimony to how Kevin Touhey's philosophy and approach to coaching is successful even in the most challenging of circumstances.

—**AL GOLDEN, HEAD FOOTBALL COACH, TEMPLE UNIVERSITY**

The Agony of Winning is a must read for the female athlete. As the coach of the number one girls' travel softball team in the state of Michigan, I have relied on the strategies Kevin lays out in the book to bond the team as an effective unit. We have always been successful, but winning is fun again because we have applied the tenets from the book. No more agony in our program, just joyful competition.

—MIKE GILLETTE, HEAD GIRLS' SOFTBALL COACH,
MICHIGAN ATHLETICS 18 UNDER

This book has put 10 years on my coaching career. In *The Agony of Winning*, Kevin provides a comprehensive strategy for players, coaches, and parents so that they can enjoy the journey and stay in the process of competing on a day to day basis. This book will change the way athletics is perceived in America, to something more fun and less stressful.

—MICHELE SHARP, HEAD WOMENS' BASKETBALL COACH, KEAN UNIVERSITY

As the Executive Director of the summer American Youth Basketball Tour, I found Kevin's book to be a wonderful tool to help guide coaches, parents, and players on what the true overall experience of competing and being part of a team should consist of. The concepts in the book that address integrity, leadership, compassion, unselfishness, appreciation, support, and contributing character during the process of competing need to by engrained in all athletic endeavors. This book is a must read for all coaches, parents, and players.

—DENNY PARKS, EXECUTIVE DIRECTOR, AMERICAN YOUTH BASKETBALL TOUR

When youth sports are focused on winning, then evaluation and critique become the focus of adult child conversations after each contest. Touhey highlights the harmful effect this has on the young athlete. As a parent and coach, his book offers practical advice on how to keep the focus on the real reasons our children should learn from sports.

—DAN APPLEGATE, PHD., PARENT OF A 6TH GRADE ATHLETE

KEVIN M. TOUHEY

THE AGONY OF WINNING

SEVEN STRATEGIES FOR WINNING BIGGER WITH GREATER FREEDOM, SPIRIT, AND INTEGRITY

Dedication

This book is dedicated to my brother Dennis Touhey. My brother Dennis coached youth baseball and football in our hometown of Dover, N.J., for 15 seasons. Like all youth coaches, he volunteered his time and energy to the young athletes under his tutelage. However, Dennis had an uncanny understanding of the fact that it was the well-being of his players and their personal growth that were most important. To be sure, his teams won a large percentage of their games. He just knew that winning was not as important as who they were becoming as young athletes. Now all of those young men who played for him are adults. I have witnessed their respect and love for my brother when they run into him. It is heartwarming for me because I have always respected the way Dennis coached, and of course I love him; he is my brother, after all.

Contents

Foreword

By Alfred Golden
Head Football Coach
Temple University

More than a half-century ago, Albert Einstein asserted, *"Concern for man and his fate must always form the chief interest of all technical endeavors – never forget this in the midst of your diagrams and equations."* As a coach, mentor, educator, and someone who has recently undertaken life's supreme challenge – fatherhood – I believe that those of us who enter the coaching arena have an obligation to teach participants more than simply how to win games. Inside *The Agony of Winning*, Kevin Touhey lays out comprehensive strategies for coaches, players, and parents, who perhaps serve as the greatest challenge facing youth sports in the 21st century. Coach Touhey's approach ensures that critical life lessons are not lost amid the competitive nature of sports and remain the central theme of youth instruction.

In *The Agony of Winning*, best-selling author and life coach Kevin Touhey illustrates how attitudes, optimism, and life-skill development translate into success for coaches, players, and parents while not requiring one to sacrifice winning. As the head football coach of a program that transformed from one win in 2006 to nine wins and our first bowl game in thirty years in 2009, I can share with you that it was our unwavering commitment to executing a process both on and off the field where core values and life-skill development served as the foundation that resulted in this cultural transformation. The 2009 Temple Football Owls are a testimony to how Kevin Touhey's philosophy and approach to coaching is successful even in the most challenging of circumstances.

The book describes useful anecdotes about how coaches and parents can make athletics fun again! The essence of training, preparation, skill development, and pushing yourself should be enjoyment and personal fulfillment. It does not have to be drudgery. Kevin steadfastly believes that this feeling needs to be restored in organized sports and needs to commence at the youth level. The essence of competition itself is in reality fun. Tennis Coach and renowned mental coach W. Timothy Gallwey, in *The Inner Game of Tennis*, points out that the three cornerstones of the Inner Game are performance, learning, and <u>enjoyment.</u> Far too often in structured sports, participants put performance first; consequently, learning, and enjoyment are sacrificed. Like Gallwey, Coach Touhey posits that if youth coaching focused more on learning, life-skill development, and enjoyment, participants would not only perform better, they would also be happier and more successful.

Coach Touhey believes youth sports are increasingly over-coached and over-regulated. The spirit of sport and its core values needs to be reintroduced as the focal point in youth sports. We need more cooperation, values-based teachings, and skill development at the youth level. Beginning with the introduction of athletics, young people need to understand

respect for the game, their teammates, coaches, c
how to make learning and competition fun onc

Inside, Kevin Touhey articulates how the incorpo..
intrinsic and extrinsic goals provides a backdrop for athle..
ics to be a valuable teaching tool for life skills and personal
development. Coaches, players, and parents, now more than
ever, have a responsibility to ensure both types of goals are
being emphasized. I would like to share with you a quotation
that I distribute annually to my staff from Basketball Hall of
Fame Coach Morgan Wooten, that reminds us all of the true
calling of coaching young people:

> *"Coaches at every level have a tendency to lose sight of
> their purpose at times, especially after success arrives.
> They start to put the cart before the horse by working
> harder and harder to develop their teams, using their
> boys to do it, gradually forgetting that their real purpose
> should be to develop the kids, using their teams to do it."*

UCLA Basketball Coach John Wooden defined success as
*"the peace of mind which is a direct result of self-satisfaction
in knowing you did your best to become the best that you are
capable of becoming."* It seems that at the youth level, both
coaches and parents have progressively lost sight of the influence that sports, particularly youth sports, can have on
character development and life skills. Instead, there has been
a gradual shift among parents and youth coaches in the last
twenty years from process-oriented to merely product (outcome) driven. Coach Wooden espoused that developing successful teams and players must instill core values comparable
to cooperation, enthusiasm, team spirit, and friendship. Values reminiscent of those presented by Coach Wooden's cel-

ebrated Pyramid of Success are noticeably absent from many youth leagues across America. Kevin Touhey believes that if these values served as the foundation of the most successful coach of the 20th century, they most assuredly must be woven into the dugouts, courts, rinks, and fields of our nation's most precious resource – our children.

Introduction

The Agony of What?

First things first: How does the word *Agony* end up in the same sentence with the word *Winning?* I can almost hear the incredulous athletes, coaches, and parents now; "The Agony of Winning? What in the heck does that mean? Aren't sports all about winning? Isn't the point of practicing and training to assure winning, to win? How can winning be agony?"

Someone who finds this volume on the bookstore shelf while browsing books on peak performance and ways to get a competitive edge will probably think it got shelved in the wrong place. It must be misguided. It might even be dangerous. Read it and before you know it, the fun of training, practicing and playing games may creep back into the serious business of sports. And it is serious business! How did we arrive at The Agony of Winning?

Just ask the 6-year-olds in full pads practicing five days a week in the August sun, or the soccer player trying to balance her travel-team schedule with her basketball practices, or the gymnast who's spent her life on the uneven parallel bars for that one shot at the Olympics. *Don't worry, honey, your first period will come when you're in your twenties. Oh yeah, so will your first date.*

Sports are no place for fun and games. Fun is not copacetic with being numero uno. Scholarship, all-conference, all-state, all-America, player of the year—there's serious stuff at stake here, a once-in-a-lifetime chance you can't afford to blow. Competition is a killer instinct that coaches and parents have instilled in young athletes almost from the time they're old enough to walk. There is no agony in winning, right? The idea of competing while having fun sounds as if it will smother that killer instinct, right? If all the athletes are walking around smiling and enjoying themselves, who will make sure we win? It is important that we instill in all our athletes that "second place is no place."

So maybe no coaches, parents, or players will dare pick up this book. It may even be banned by Little League, US Soccer, and the NCAA. Maybe they'll light the post-pep-rally bonfire by tossing this sacrilegious stack of paper on top of the pile of wood.

But I hope some of them will read it instead. Because – let me make this clear – I love sports, absolutely, truly, and deeply. I love the real essence of competition, whatever the venue. I have written *The Agony of Winning* because I care tremendously about protecting the good that athletic competition can do. I know without a doubt that we have moved far away from the original, true spirit of sport, and we're moving farther away all the time. I have written this book to show the way back.

What do I mean by "the spirit of sport?" What is it we've lost that I want to help restore? It's the love of the game, yes, but it's more than that – it is an inner fire, a vibrant source of energy within the soul of the athlete that doesn't depend on anyone or anything else. In this spirit, training for competition is a personal learning experience whose most important lessons have to do not with playing your best, but with *being* your best. What matters most isn't the big win, but the journey you take to get there, and what the journey teaches you about yourself.

When all the emphasis is placed on who is No. 1, or how much money the next contract will bring – when people really believe that second place is no place – almost all those who compete are going to end up losers. The internal combustion ignited by the process of training to compete and the fun of actually playing in a game turns into an iceberg the moment when the desired outcome does not occur. The true spirit of sport is not tied to outcomes – to winning, losing, scholarships, or any other external measure of athletic success. This doesn't mean that so-called outcome goals don't matter, it just means that they don't matter the *most*. If anything, it's the true spirit of sport that makes our outcomes more satisfying and lets us enjoy them to their fullest.

Don't get me wrong – I love winning. And I'm not some frustrated armchair athlete who always got picked last on the playground or never made varsity. I have been a winner my entire life, starting with my playing days and continuing into my coaching career. Since leaving the college coaching arena, I have built a successful practice as a life coach and inspirational speaker. In 2008, I became an Amazon.com best-selling author when my first book, *The Miracle of Optimism,* reached

No. 2 on the Hot New Releases list, as well as No. 3 out of all the books in its category in the country. But now I realize that what I learned about myself on that journey, through the doubts and fears, exhaustion and exhilaration of bringing the book to publication, was more valuable than that outcome, too. The nuggets of wisdom I uncovered while writing the book, the ones I use to live a vibrant life – the real diamonds – were mined along the way.

The **Strategies** I have put forth in the lessons and exercises have been developed over 52 years of involvement with athletics. (If nothing else, my approach has longevity!) I am truly blessed to have had so many different experiences in the arena of sports – as a player, as a coach, as an athletic Peak Performance Professional, and now as an older parent of young children who are having a ball in youth soccer and basketball. And, looking back at my own childhood, I see that I was lucky to see both sides of athletics so early on – both the exhilaration and the spirit-crushing expectations.

I believe the potential for personal growth through athletics – for players, parents, and coaches alike – is limitless. But that potential is not being realized because the current state of athletic programs in communities, schools, and colleges is an inadequate delivery system for the lessons that sports have to teach. Too many coaches, parents, and players are taking shortcuts around the lessons, reading the CliffsNotes. In the meantime, the spirit of sport is being buried beneath over-commitment, over-coaching, and over-organization. *The Agony of Winning* is an archaeological expedition to bring to light that buried wisdom – the real diamonds we find on the journey. In the chapters ahead, we'll examine seven of these diamonds; succinct Strategies for taking a more enlightened approach to sports, with stories to illustrate them along with lessons and exercises to help you integrate them into your own life.

The world of athletics is chock full of players, parents, and coaches hell-bent on striving against one another, struggling at all costs to attain *their* goal of being No. 1 and meanwhile trampling all over the real gifts of sport. We need to stop and take an honest look at what we are putting ourselves through in the name of competition. We need to look, for example, at why coaches on all levels are working unprecedented hours in the name of winning; how "professional" the world of collegiate athletes is becoming; and, why pro sports has become nothing but big business. We need to look at how parents, in pushing their children relentlessly to succeed, have driven today's young athletes into a kind of burnout that sports has never seen. I believe the 7 Strategies in this book, if applied thoughtfully and diligently, will help us build a stable structure for a sports world that's in danger of spinning out of control.

How many heart-wrenching stories have to be revealed before those of us in the world of sports learn something new about winning? How many coaches and athletes need to fall victim to the Agony of Winning? One more is too many.

Winning

The Thrill is Gone

"Spanning the globe to bring you the constant variety of sport . . . the thrill of Victory (winning) and agony of defeat . . . the human drama of athletic competition . . . This is ABC's Wide World of Sports." That was the opening, spoken by Jim McKay, of the long-running sports show, "The Wide World of Sports." In many ways, Jim McKay was the man that made sports come alive for me in my youth. Long before the increased sports coverage by ESPN and 24-hour sports networks, there were only a few sports shows to keep fans hungry for the coverage that would satisfy our desire for sports information. "Wide World of Sports" was only on once a week, so the anticipation of the next segment was great. The drama of the show was the actual competition of the games. The competition and contests featured provided the backdrop for the thrill of winning or the agony of defeat, not whether or not the participants were dating Jessica Simpson, or calculating the precise number of lovers that Tiger Woods bedded. I mean, I did not know anyone who did not watch "Wide World of Sports."

I have worked with some top athletes over the years as a Peak Performance Life Coach. Lauren Edelschien was one of the top tennis players at Rutgers University in New Jersey when she became a client of mine in 2006. She had been a competitive tennis player, like her mother before her, since she was a little girl. She had experienced the thrill of winning and agony of defeat since the day she started eating real food, or at least that is what it seemed like to her. The side effects of winning and more specifically the relentless drive to be THE No. 1 player eventually led to her not being able to handle food. As a young woman, competing on scholarship at Rutgers, the burden and expectations of being No. 1 at all times took their toll on her spirit. By the time Lauren came to me, her tennis game was suffering under the pressure she had lived under since the racket was taller than she was. She felt her life, her daily schedule, her freedom belonged to everyone and everything but her. She developed bulimia as a way to be in control of something. Throwing up as much as nine times a day seemed to give her the power over herself that was absent in other areas of her life.

Lauren's parents are wonderful people. I have worked with the families of thousands of athletes, but the Edelschien family is one of my all-time favorites. That statement speaks to the long-established fact that bad things happen to good people.

I think what makes this case so important is that the pressure Lauren felt was more covert than overt. Her mom and dad absolutely thought they were providing Lauren with what she wanted and Lauren was thinking she did not want to disappoint her parents. Lauren and her parents cared about each other, but they did not hear each other.

Lauren felt that her parents' commitment of time, effort, and expense required her to continue playing even though her passion for the game was waning. She was actually in survivor's mode by the time we met. She was on a full scholarship to play tennis at Rutgers, the desired goal of all those years of travel to tournaments, private lessons, and entry fees paid. Those results included a full athletic scholarship, tournament championships, and trophies on the mantel, so why was the Agony of Winning so prevalent for Lauren? She had made it, so why was she suffering? Over time, Lauren had found a secret way to relieve the pressure to perform. It gave her some morsel of power and control. With the same intensity of her tennis serve, Lauren served herself meals that were more than her small anatomy could handle. Lauren would devour a whole cake with the same vigor she would down an opponent with her tennis forehand. The emotional release of acing the opponent, however, was no match for huddling over the toilet bowl and purging that chocolate cake she inhaled faster than she could say 40–love.

The first thing I did was give Lauren the permission to quit playing tennis. Yes, to save her life, I thought it was best for her to stop playing tennis. We met with her parents. The love they demonstrated for her in that meeting was a privilege to witness. They were on board with my advice, even if it meant Lauren lost her scholarship for the coming school year.

The good news is that Lauren completely recovered and has come along with me on some speaking engagements and shared her story with other top athletes. **The Strategies for Winning with Freedom, Spirit, and Integrity** were fully adopted by Lauren. She worked hard on all the **Strategies** that eventually became this book. These methods produce fierce competitors, who either rediscover their passion for sport or find it for the first time. Those who employ the strategies contained in this book are in the zone: winning athletes, coaches, and parents. They learn to look beyond the wins and the losses for the life lessons that competition can teach them.

I believe it is important for the readers of this book to see the final results of Lauren's career as a college tennis player. She enthusiastically competed as the No. 3 player on the Rutgers University Tennis Team in her senior year.

I received the following e-mail from her in her l;st year at Rutgers:

Hey Coach T!

I just wanted to let you know everything is going great... Tennis is unbelievable! I can't believe how well these tools have worked for me every time I step out onto the court. I just get my mind in a zone where I focus on my tennis and it seems as if nothing could stand in the way. I won both of my singles and doubles match this past week vs. Army and Seton Hall! I would love if you could catch a match at some point during the season. My dad came up to watch and we talked for awhile afterwards and he asked how the techniques work on the court and he could tell right away how focused and determined I was. I was down in one of my matches and I fought back to win the battle. Every point is its own separate point now and that helps me to believe in myself and know that I can play out there for hours if that is what it takes to win! I hope all is well at home for you! I bet you're busy so don't work tooo hard!

Take care and see you soon!

Lauren Edelshein,
Rutgers University Tennis Player 2006-2007

In the last 20 years we have gone from the thrill of winning to the agony of winning at an alarming rate. The outcomes that we thought were the end result, the ones we strived so much for, are no longer providing that thrill of winning, at least not for long. I sense an extreme overreaction to losing or not performing well in the work I do with coaches, parents, and the athletes themselves. However, equally alarming is that I am witnessing a very muted emotional response to winning — no real joy or goal satisfaction. Great performances are met with a "is that all there is to it" kind of response. I hear coaches and athletes lament that they had worked so hard toward the game day competition and then it was over and the focus very quickly became about what's next.

Athletics has become an arms race of athletic competition increasingly rooted in the "hey, what's next?" mentality, about questioning if the next thing will be bigger and better than what was just experienced. Make no mistake about it, winning feels better than losing, and it is supposed to; however, there is more to it than meets the eye. Reducing sports to being all about winning is an extremely small criterion to measure the whole of the athletic experience against. To be sure, the agony of winning beats the agony of defeat. However, this book is about restoring the concept of the Thrill of Winning. Agony is such a descriptive word. Agony impacts two important levels of the human psyche both emotionally and mentally. The stress level of athletes, parents, and coaches is directly linked to this attitude that the outcome is the only important measuring stick of success in sports.

I worked with Olympic-caliber gymnast Darlene Hill from New Jersey, and she was in agony. We applied the Agony of Winning principles just to keep her energy level to where she could continue to compete. Darlene was a poster child for the Agony of Winning. She was a champion gymnast in every sense of the word. She would train and train for the meets and after a routine was over and scores, usually very high, were posted, she would describe her feelings as relief, not joy. The winning was kind of anticlimactic. She had competed with fear in her heart over whether she would live up to the expectations of those around her. There was little joy for her. After all, the main focus was on more training because there would be another tournament the next weekend, and all of a sudden the fact that she won didn't matter. This is really sad. A few days before she was to compete at the Wachovia Center in Philadelphia for a spot on the Olympic team, she sat in my living room with me and cried. Darlene Hill was broken. Her mind, body, and spirit were shattered under years of training and high expectations. She had been victorious enough to be labeled a sure shot for the team. However, she was in agony. It did not matter to this 18-year-old who had been training for this moment for nine years whether she made the team. That is the Agony of Winning.

She told me the only reason she kept competing was because she did not want to let down those around her – her family, her dedicated coaches. and the other young gymnasts who looked up to her. It is difficult to stay motivated when there are no intrinsic passions driving the athlete. This is the most graphic case I have ever had of an athlete having no internal source of inspiration for competing. As Darlene often told me, "Only about one percent of my drive to compete is for me, the other ninety-nine percent is for others, to not let them down." This type of attitude is a breeding ground for the Agony of Winning. Her story is not an isolated case of burnout but rather is an example of what is becoming the norm in sports.

It is important to speed up delivery of the Strategies in this book, to incorporate **Strategy One: Agony of Winning Triangle: The Who, What, and Why of Athletics** at warp speed. The time is right to set aside the time to emphasize the process and journey side of athletic participation. It is time to state that we are selling short the potential lifelong teaching benefit of athletics. So much emphasis is on getting to the end so we can see if the scoreboard says we are winners ... or losers.

Where is the process of measuring the small increments of participation? What do those small measurements tell us about why we play and who we are while we play? Chris Carr, a sports psychologist in Indianapolis, Ind., says, *"If we focus too much on the outcome, we lose the opportunity to get better through the process. We need to educate people how to manage the short-term goals like getting the play right, the execution. If you focus on those things and use those as measurements, then oftentimes you can have success even though you didn't win. If you only focus on the outcome, you miss the opportunity to get better."* Carr is on the right track; however, his statement is still referring to the "what" or technical skills side of athletic participation.

He is commenting on the extrinsic measurements. But at least he is talking about the process, the journey. It is time for those involved with sports to train themselves to deliver a message that includes lessons larger than simply getting ready for the next game. It must include lessons about leadership, self-awareness and improvement, a commitment to fair play, relationships, sportsmanship, and learning about accountability and personal responsibility.

Athletics is always about working on oneself, not the opponent. Gary Bennett is a sports psychologist at Virginia Tech. He says, "At Virginia Tech, there's significant emphasis on respect." Bennett continues: "Respecting the opponent, respecting the game, athletes who are winning can still learn the importance of continually developing this type of respect, which, hopefully, also helps develop a measure of humility." I could not agree more. The important thing to understand is that the goal of winning is not going to be sacrificed on the altar of emphasizing the more intrinsic values of sports. It has been my experience that individuals encouraged to embrace intrinsic value-based goals play on teams that do the same, and they win. They also tend to experience The Thrill of Winning more readily. These teams have sought the solutions to the Agony of Winning that I am presenting in this book. They tend to process the pressure of competing more readily. The end result often ends up being a winning team that also enjoys the process and journey of athletic competition. Isn't it ironic that teams who do not make the ultimate purpose of participation the big "W" end up with more "W's" and enjoying it more?

When working with Lauren and Darlene, my entire process was based on reducing their stress. The Agony of Winning was prevalent for them because they had no real joy left for competing. The stress they felt led them down a path to burnout. The Agony of Winning was arrived at through too many games, too soon, too many expectations, without any attachment to the spirit of sport. It is never too late to begin teaching the methods found within the **Seven Strategies** of this book, which take participants on a journey from the Agony of Winning to the thrill. I have encountered many individuals and teams who had lost their zeal for playing – the Agony of Winning Strategies helped restore their passion for competition.

By the time athletes are in high school and college they have played and trained so much that the thrill of winning has become as mundane as their endless training. So ultimately all that striving and training, such as that Lauren and Darlene experienced, led them to the same destination: the "Agony of Winning."

This agony is a direct result of too much training, training too young, having too much coaching, too much parental involvement, too many practices, too many games and tournaments, too many awards, too much of everything, and much too soon.

The time has come for the world of sports – parents, coaches, and players – to pay attention to the lessons the Agony of Winning has been trying to teach us for years. You will find on the pages of this book the remedy for restoring the Thrill of Winning. You may be surprised how simple that restoration process can be.

What is needed to remedy The Agony of Winning is some compassion-driven athletes.

Concept for transforming the Agony of Winning to the Thrill of Winning:

The day- to-day process or journey of training is the destination. This is where the life lessons can be found and taught on an ongoing basis. This is where the thrill resides. Too much emphasis is placed on the outcome in today's world of sports.

～～～

Question for transforming the Agony of Winning to the Thrill of Winning:

What steps could you, as a player, coach, or parent take, to assure that you are paying more attention to the step-by-step process of practicing and training? What are you willing to do to let go of outcome- based participation to focus your goals on in-the-moment experiences and what those experiences are trying to teach you, about yourself?

～～～

Word for Transforming the Agony of Winning to the Thrill of Winning:

Intrinsic

2

The Lofty Potential of Compassion-Driven Athletics

Compassion-driven athletics requires a deep awareness of the process and journey of athletics. Compassion means that you are in a state of being deeply aware, full of care for the process and the journey, while you seek to attain your goal. The Agony of Winning has become so prevalent because we have come to a place in sports where only the outcome is important. We have to put some feeling back into the mix. Compassion does just that; it adds some positive emotion into the world of competitive athletics. Competing with compassion means paying attention to the process of training and the playing of each game, not just the end result. It means paying attention to how you are behaving and who you are becoming along the way, while you seek the results. That's where the diamonds are found. The beautiful thing is that we do not need to sacrifice winning, not one bit. In fact, when I first stared writing this book I envisioned the title as "Competing with Compassion." However, I realized that people were in Agony, even when victorious, and that compassion-based athletics was the cure for that Agony. So I changed the book's title to reflect the challenge and realized the cure lay in a compassionate approach to athletics. That approach would provide the solution for parents, coaches, and players.

Why are parents, coaches, and especially the athletes in Agony? One reason is because the delivery system in the modern era begins much earlier in the life of an athlete than in past years. The athletes are younger and are being placed dangerously in the path of the agenda of their undertrained youth coaches. Winning is the agenda of many of these adult coaches. I had a bird's-eye view of this while coaching my daughter in a recreational league for third and fourth graders. This story underscores the foundational reasons for the Agony of Winning.

Ed Maroon, the volunteer commissioner and a good man, came under fire from a group of parent/coaches about the pairings for the playoffs for these girls. In a series of e-mails he received, he was basically accused of rigging the seeding system for the playoffs. The reason he would want to fix the seeding in his favor, according to the parent/coaches who were upset, was the fact that he also coached one of the teams his daughter was on. He received e-mails letting him know that there were seeding errors. Several coaches pointed out that the errors were significant and would alter the brackets in this important playoff system. Some e-mails asked Ed if he had the power to set the final standings without regard to the teams' records. One coach suggested that Ed would manipulate the standings if it benefited him. The team I coached had won one single game. One! Yet I had a blast coaching. My players, one of whom was my daughter, had fun, too. But these top-rung coaches were wallowing in The Agony of Winning over their seeding in the playoffs, for third and fourth graders.

In an email, where one parent wrote how she wanted to demonstrate righteousness for her daughter, that she was showing her third-grader that standing up to the seeding debacle represented a lesson learned about doing the right thing. In an e-mail, I suggested that none of the girls, including her daughter, really understood anything about seeding for the playoffs. Sarcastically, I wrote that if I mentioned seeding to my third-grader she might have responded that it was a little early to start planting the grass. She might have said, "Dad, isn't seeding something we do in the spring?" There are many more relevant lessons these parents might have delivered to their charges, lessons about having fun, and being good teammates and good sports. These are important lessons for the youth of America.

So, the volunteer commissioner eventually sent this e-mail to all of us. He was obviously in Agony, despite the fact that his team had finished in first place. He was not affected by the seeding at all.

WOW!

Thank you all for the emails. To clarify how the seeding was decided, it was simply done as it appeared on the website. It may not have been a perfect system, but I have decided to keep it that way. It really will not make a bit of difference. Again, this is not the world championship of G34 basketball. I did not look at score or anything like that; this is not the BSC Bowl scoring system. I am sorry if everyone does not agree with that, but for the sake of simplicity, that is how I am going to keep it. I have spent the better part of four months making sure that everything was well planned so that the girls would have a great experience. To say that I would manipulate anything to my advantage is outrageous. This is not about me or for that matter any of you. It is about the girls.

It is very important that we keep what's important here, and that is the girls. This is a REC. league not a travel league. It is meant to be fun and educational. We have some very talented girls as well as some girls that have never played before. The last thing we want to do is send a message that it is OK to not play by the rules or to turn someone off to a sport. Again, we are not talking about high school or NBA rules.

I realize that this may upset some of you, and I am truly sorry. I hope that everyone has a great play-off season and best wishes.

Ed Maroon

Wow was the correct response. All these coaches are good people who volunteer their time generously. However, they fell victim to this phenomenon of winning not being enough. Thus, they were in Agony over the playoff system. I also hopped into the discussion again after a few more accusatory e-mails were fired at Ed. I wrote:

"Oh my God is all I can say. I write and speak for a living and this dialog has me speechless and I do not know what to write. Holy mackerel, is this all that important?

You know what would be fun, put all the numbers in a hat and pull them out to match the teams. I want the top team first!!!

I have a better idea, no playoffs, no standings, no ALL Star game. These are young kids. If you want to make it more important than it should be then keep up the kind of attitude that is reflected in these messages.

I have been the Life Coach for hundreds of athletes in this school district over the past 8 years ages 16-22 who have had it with sports because since they were 6, 7, 8, 9 years old they have already played in 100's of games, playoffs, all star games etc. etc. By the way, these are the athletes you all read about in the paper. You would be surprised at some of the names

Come on guys, lighten up. I don't care if Ed is cheating, or any other coach is cheating and I am not saying they are, just that it does not matter to me On my team Maria, Sarah, Olivia, Tessa, Tara, and Delaney have improved tremendously. That's what is important, and they had fun.

Our goal was that they could not wait for Tuesdays and Thursdays. Those were our practice days.

When I read these messages it is clear to me that the kids are not the priority because they could give a darn about all this stuff, unless you are making it important to them."

The goal of being the best remains an honorable one. We just need to remember that athletics' most important lessons are found along the way. What's more, we don't have to wait till the end of the road to measure "being the best." There are mile markers throughout the journey, if you're watching. And often you'll find what you're looking for in the potholes and wrong turns. When Brett Favre, future NFL Hall of Fame quarterback, was asked for his favorite memory of his playing career, he said, "The funny thing is, it's not about the touchdowns and big victories. If I were to make a list, I would include the interceptions, the sacks, and the really painful losses. Those times when I've been kicked around, I hold on to those. In a way, those are the best times I've ever had, because that's when I've found out who I am and what I want to be."

I believe the potential benefits of athletics lie in its ability to teach major life lessons to all participants. The potential for coaches, parents, and players to upgrade their leadership and communication skills knows no bounds. However, athletics is tremendously underused as a tool for personal and professional growth. The potential to use athletic participation as if it were a classroom and to enhance personal growth can be profound. However, the delivery system of present-day athletics is not living up to its vast capacity to teach. Just like in the classroom, participants need to open their books and pay attention to the lessons. And those lessons must be taught with vigor. What is occurring today reminds me of a talented athlete who does not live up to his potential. He or she goes through the motions, just getting by but never live up to their greatest potential.

We can ensure that we alleviate the Agony of Winning by paying attention to the journey and the process. The following e-mail to me came from a parent after I threw in my two cents:

Kevin,

I couldn't agree with you more. Mel and I have tried teaching our girls as much as we could and are still trying to keep it fun. We had a girl who wanted to quit the first week, but by the third week couldn't wait to come to practice. She improved tremendously and even smiles when she scores or rebounds the ball. We won some games in the beginning, but lost the last several games because other teams kept everyone past the three point arch. Some of the parents weren't happy that we didn't do the same, but we explained to them as nicely as we could that we were going to teach fundamentals, not play chess or 1 on 1 games. It is a team sport and everyone gets to dribble, pass, and shoot. As long as the kids have fun, learn, and continue to want to play the game after the season is over that's what is important.

Thanks for your original email.

Patti Lynn Monaghan

These parents are like hundreds of other parents who have put sports in the proper perspective. When coaches/parents become aware of where the Agony of Winning is rooted, it becomes easy to coach and teach athletes to compete with compassion. There is so much more to the learning process in sports than the scores of the games.

Putting the emphasis on athletics as an educational experience takes some time away from practice, but it is worth it in the long run. The full potential of sports can be arrived at by teaching a new way of winning, one that brings with it joy and happiness, rather than Agony. However, it is a process, and it starts with the coach emphasizing the right things and educating parents and players alike. The following letter is a step toward relieving the Agony of Winning:

Dear Parents,

I just wanted to drop a note to let you know I am proud to be coaching your daughter. I am positive we will be the underdog in most of the games this year. That is really fine with me. The most important days of the week for your children are Tuesdays and Wednesdays. We do not use those practice days to get ready to play a game, we use it to teach them the basics of the basketball, get a great workout, learn to compete, and mostly have fun.

We play a lot of 3 on 3 in practice so ALL the girls get to touch the ball, pass the ball, dribble the ball and shoot the ball. That takes up a lot of practice time but it is important to me that they all have a chance to improve.

I do this rather than put in a bunch of plays that favor a girl or two. If we did that we may win a few more games but the good players on our team will not really get better, and those who need to improve the most will not get the valuable practice time they need to improve their skills.

So please reinforce to your children that Tuesdays and Wednesdays are the most important days. This does not mean that we will not teach competition; however winning games is less important right now than their overall experience of learning the game and having fun. So many children stop playing sports because of a bad experience at ages 7, 8, and 9.

I just wanted you to know that I love sports and I love coaching your children, but the emphasis is in the wrong place in youth sports and I am going to contribute to the change. I am counting on you helping me do that.

Sincerely,

Kevin M. Touhey

When coaches take time to communicate to parents and athletes that winning isn't everything, it is widely accepted. From my experience conducting workshops for all age groups, youth through college, the participants are excited about getting some relief from the Agony of Winning. They want a system that promotes a different approach to winning, a system with more meaning, because the process is a vehicle to infuse a more values-based approach to the playing and coaching experience. I can tell you from experience that these methods and strategies are welcomed and very teachable.

Applying The Agony of Winning principles will instill a more wholesome approach early in the careers of coaches and athletes. Then we can assure that participation holds an educational component that teaches respect, sportsmanship, the building of healthy relationships, and more.

In the fall 2009 edition of the "NCAA Champion" magazine, Executive Director David Pickle made some interesting points in his editorial. He notes that we are in danger of losing the connection between education and sports. He writes the following: "For those who believe in educationally based athletics, this is a troubling case because so few people involved seem to see a direct correlation between athletics and education." He continues: "The regrettable fact is that high school (and college) athletics programs have lost their way at times, leaving the door open to critics who assert that a sport is not really a complement to education. I can say that this is very troubling. We have record participation in sports today from the college level all the way down to youth leagues. It is a perfect opportunity to use it as a vehicle to teach the participants to be better people not just better athletes."

In the same article Tim Flannery, assistant director for the National Federation of State High School Associations, says, "Other than our best coaches, most people don't really believe athletics is educational in nature." This is a very dangerous attitudinal shift regarding the role that athletics should play in the educational community. This attitude has given birth to the whole pay-to-play movement in youth sports, which is not a good thing."

The NFHS and I have the same belief, that sports do not inherently teach athletes anything. They believe, and I agree, that we need to spend the time to teach the lessons, open the book, and stop reading the CliffsNotes. The NFHS, almost ironically, is challenging the notion that sports build character. Instead, the organization has taken the position that sports builds character only if character development is taught as part of the experience. Schools are the logical place for such instructions to occur, but success will result only if major changes are made at the base level of American sports.

The working definition of compassion-based athletics means caring enough to do what Pickle and Flannery are suggesting sports should do, which is to teach something other than just winning and losing. The **Seven Strategies** in this book do just that. They provide a process and formula for capturing the essence of what sports has to teach. Winning will again be a thrill if we include the whole of the athletic experience and not just focus on the results of the game.

Integrating The Agony of Winning strategies will have a positive effect on the way we look at sports in our society today. These principles will help athletes compete with compassion, cherish the spirit in sports, and demonstrate that it is more than the final score that matters. The intense pressure to win, to be No. 1, is distorting the beauty of sports. That pressure has filtered down to the youngest athletes. Because we live in an era where the only acceptable outcome is not just winning, but being No. 1, the life lessons necessary for true personal awareness and ultimate success as a human being are being obliterated. This obsession for athletic perfection drains the fun for everyone involved. This phenomenon seems to have become more and more prevalent, especially over the last 20 years.

What would sports be like if each person tapped into the spirit within and competed with enthusiasm and a passionate drive for success, win or lose? What would it be like if coaches on all levels used the time necessary to ensure that when losing occurred, it was forgotten quickly, and when winning was achieved, it was a thrill? That is what this book is about. The strategies are about how to do that. As I will demonstrate, there is a succinct manner in which to change Agony back to Thrill. It all starts with **Strategy One,** which states that coaches will designate time to incorporate the principles of the Agony of Winning. This time allotment to teach life lessons is the bedrock strategy that the other **Six Strategies** are built upon, and with parents reinforcing the principles we are on our way to solving the Agony of Winning challenge. It is a challenge that parents, coaches, and players are ready to welcome.

This message came from a grateful parent:

Coach Kevin

Thank you for this note. You are a breath of fresh air. We have four children and our oldest was turned off to baseball in only third grade by one of the meanest coaches in history. We forced him to play in fourth just so he could leave on a positive note. Lucky for him, he has had coaches since then with the same philosophy as you. He started to enjoy himself, learn, and then continued to play.

Nicole loves to play basketball. It should be a lot of fun to watch all of the girls improve while they have fun.

Take care,

Trish Emerle

And this one:

Thanks Coach - Delaney is very excited to be on your team. The greatest joy was watching Delaney sink a foul shot - something she was so frustrated with all last year. It's all she talked about this weekend - not the fact that they lost. I love your philosophy, and we are all looking forward to watching our girls play this year, win or lose. Thank you so much for coaching and for the email. See you Tuesday.

Kris Watson

What will the new perspective on athletics look like when a system like the one I established in countless youth, high school, and college programs – of setting Intrinsic and Extrinsic goals that are measurable – is in place? When an athletic program decides an Agony of Winning Code of Ethics that includes integrity and respect as tenets is vitally important, wouldn't that help relieve the stress of participation? Wouldn't we have a more vibrant, energetic, joyful system if we incorporated the Agony of Winning strategy of putting in place a system that taught **Core Values** and held its participants accountable for them? The **Pressure to Succeed** has certainly lent a hand to participants feeling the Agony of Winning. What if a strategy was employed that taught how **Letting go of the Outcome** and focusing on the process, preparation and having fun could be better?

In addition, it is important to teach how the loss of focus is due to letting the day-to-day **Distractions** of life affect our concentration. As focus increases, pressure decreases. I know coaches and players would welcome a system to help with laser beam concentration, now wouldn't they? These are all teachable concepts laid out in the following chapters. And I add other **Strategies** such as *Competing with Purpose and Passion* and *Setting Intrinsic as well as Extrinsic Goals.*

I also coach youth soccer. That is another hotbed for the Agony of Winning and a wonderful place to begin *Setting a Tone for Integrity, Respect, and Civility.*

However, I wanted to be sure you understand that as a youth coach it was easy for me to talk about the basketball playoff system because we had one only one game. The solutions I offer for compassion-based athletics are applicable win or lose. Following is an e-mail that was sent to my wife Annabelle from Elaine Monaco who is a parent of one of my youth soccer players.

> *"I love Kevin's coaching abilities. There are not many coaches out there like him. The way he spoke to the girls and tried to teach them the way the world __should__ go around with sports was amazing. The team won a lot of games 'without keeping score' but they also learned the true importance of being an athlete and being part of a team."*

Wouldn't it be nice to erase the **Agony of Winning** and restore the **Thrill of Winning** for all athletes using these strategies, just like the Shawnee High School Football team and one of its greatest players, Chris La Pierre, did? The next chapter tells their story and how they put the strategies to use.

Concept for Transforming the Agony of Winning to the Thrill of Winning:

A key to process-based athletics is empathy. If we listen to the other people we are in a relationship with in athletics with compassion and civility, participation becomes less stressful.

Question for Transformation from Agony of Winning to the Thrill of Winning:

What are the most fundamental life lessons that athletic participation holds the key to? How are our actions as a parent, coach, or player in alignment with the teaching or learning of those lessons? If you are out of alignment, what are you willing to do to change that?

Word for Transforming the Agony of Winning to the Thrill of Winning:

Compassion

3

Transforming the Agony

A New Perspective for Sports

Head Football Coach Tim Gushue from Shawnee High School in New Jersey decided to change some of the emphasis in the day-to-day operation of his program. When Coach Gushue called me in September 2002 he was distressed. He was already a successful winning football coach who suffered from an extreme case of The Agony of Winning. He had won numerous conference championships and had been to the state playoffs many times, advancing to the state championship on several occasions. He just had not won the "Big Game," meaning the state championship. In fact, the year before his team had lost a heart-breaking game in the state finals. The core players from that team were returning to play another season. It seemed to everyone that Shawnee High School would make it to the state finals again, and maybe this time they would secure a win. In other words, win the Big One and relieve the Agony of all the players, coaches, and long-suffering parents. Instead, they started the season by losing their first two games. Defeat was now an ingredient added to the Agony. The Agony of Winning was now intensified by losing. The Agony of Losing can feel like a near death experience.

Coach Gushue, who is a great man and a fine leader, decided that something was missing. He knew it was not the teaching of the technical skills necessary for Winning -- it was something else, something less tangible. What I truly love about Coach Gushue is that he possessed the humility to ascertain that he needed to learn about my strategies for reaching maximum potential and transform from the Agony of Winning to the Thrill of Winning.

He asked me to explain my views on athletics and how my program could help his team achieve its goals and maintain a character-based, respectful program. I told Coach that you can break down the essence of the athletics into three aspects — the **Agony of Winning Triangle.** Its three points are technical skills, behaviors, and attitudes. Technical skills are the "what," behavior is the "who," and attitude is the "why" of athletic competition.

The technical skills, or the "what," are the basic techniques needed to accomplish the task at hand. Whether this means a coaching technique or a playing technique, it embodies "what" to do in regards to accomplishing an athletic skill set. The observable actions of an individual parent, fan, coach, or player is the "who" aspect. These are the observable behaviors being demonstrated while the participants are carrying out the technical skills they have been taught.

The last and ultimately most fundamental aspect of this is attitude, or the "why" of athletic participation. This refers to the underlying motivators for participation. Just to be clear about how I am using the word *attitude*, I mean the reasons, the core passions and interests of those involved with athletes. The reasons or the "why" someone participates is essential because this is where the spirit of sports resides. If the underlying motivation and passion for competing are not positive and energizing, participation in sports can become lifeless. This is especially true when the "what" aspect of sports is not living up to the pre-determined set of expectations. The foundation that supports the "what" when things are not going well is a solid set of positive motivations for participation. I told Coach that it would take only one session to see if the "what," "who" and "why" of his team were out of balance. Coach decided to allot time to this process and hired me to incorporate **Strategy One: Agony of Winning Triangle** to relieve some of the pain associated with the Agony of Winning. In other words, to set aside time to work on the more intrinsic values of athletic participation with the players and coaches.

My first meeting was held in the school library. It did not take much time to see that the "why" aspect of the team was out of alignment. I told Coach weekly sessions were needed to correct this problem. So Coach Gushue employed the first strategy of the Agony of Winning program and allotted the time needed. I met with the team every week that year and also every week since that year. We continue to work on the "why" in the Shawnee football program. The solutions achieved with **Strategy One** have resulted in the coaches and team reaching their full potential. It also led to four state championships in the eight years since I established the program with the Shawnee team. The Agony of Winning has been transformed to the Thrill. The "why" of the program's participation has taken hold and changed the entire culture of the program. It has become an athletic program that wins with integrity and respect and has fun doing it. The "why" and the "who" are some vitally important aspects of the success of this program.

The "why" of participation is the place from which the true, long-lasting motivations for playing come from. The "why" is an internal matter, the heart of the matter, the spirit of the matter. When the emphasis is out of balance and skewed toward the "what," athletic competition is reduced to the scores of the games. What results is that sports are relying almost exclusively on external measurements of success and motivation. Over the last 20 years, society has deemed sports success only in terms of those external markers, meaning winning or losing. In fact, in the last 10 years or so, the bar has been raised even higher. The emphasis on winning as the most desirable outcome has morphed into the point of view that being No. 1 is the only desirable outcome of athletic competition.

This causes tremendous pressure about game performance. Subsequently, more and more time is being allotted to the "what" aspects of sports to ensure that measurement of success is accomplished. When most measurements of success are external, it is impossible to tap into the true nature of competition. When there is a lack of awareness around the "why" of competing, combined with not arriving at the external expectation, we begin to witness some of the ugly occurrences we see in athletics today. The disappointment, frustration and anger levels of players, coaches, and fans when the predetermined "what" goal is not attained have reached epic proportions.

Chris La Pierre, who broke the record for touchdowns scored in the state of New Jersey, benefited in a big way from Coach Gushue's commitment to the Agony of Winning program. I conducted the weekly workshops that Chris participated in for three years. He was a star player for sure. However, in those meetings his teammates asked him for more than just his athletic prowess. They wanted to get to know him better, they wanted leadership from him, they wanted him to include and mentor the underclassmen that played behind him on the depth chart. Chris's world was chock full of achievements, awards, and trophies. He had the "what" of football down pat, in part because he had an incredible work ethic, a very honorable trait for sure. However, that work ethic mainly benefited him and the team on the "what" side. The Agony of Winning was still present for him and his teammates. Chris took the challenge and worked hard on the "why" of his participation and on the "who" he was being in regard to the rest of his teammates.

In January 2009, Chris was on a panel for a forum I conducted to address the Agony of Winning concepts. Although the panel included former NFL players Fred Barnett; the Invincible himself, Vince Papale; Dave O'Brien, the chairman of the Sports Management Department at Drexel University; and yours truly, Chris stole the show with his speech, titled the following:

The Value of Athletic Participation – It is not just Touchdowns and Goals Scored

Chris is a walking testament to the power of the Life Lessons learned in this program. He transformed the Agony of Winning to compassion-based participation. His opening remarks:

"I'd like to start off by saying thank you to Mr. Touhey for letting me speak to all of you tonight. I think it's great that our community is fortunate enough to have something like this. I know growing up through the youth programs in this area, I never had this opportunity and we are truly lucky to be able to gather and discuss sports on a level that most of us never even consider..."

The parents, student athletes, and panel members listened intently as he continued on:

"I started playing football when I was five years old. Shortly after, I was given my first baseball bat, and not too long after I started playing basketball and lacrosse. Sports have always been my life. I would jump straight from one season to another and usually even double up two or three sports at a time. I even once played in a lacrosse game wearing baseball pants because we left the baseball game early to make the lacrosse game, only to find out I left my lacrosse uniform home. It's not every day you see a kid running up and down a lacrosse field wearing pin-stripes..."

Adopting **Strategy One** requires a commitment to taking the time necessary to develop the "who" and the "why" more fully for coaches, parents, and athletes alike. We do not need to try to capture a bygone era to establish compassion-based athletics. In fact, we need a system that responds to the demands of the high-stress environment of today's world of sports. Chris's story is most prevalent today with young athletes playing on multiple teams or playing multiple sports. He is a product of the culture that holds that high-stress winning is the most important thing. However, he is also a product of the Agony of Winning system and so has learned to compete with compassion.

> *"But just like most kids, I grew up learning that it's fun when you win, but not when you lose. What I'm going to try to talk about with all of you is that sports are more than winning and losing, much more. It's more than how many points you can score and how many shots you can make. Sports are about competing because you want to compete, not competing just because you want to win. And that's when you start to wonder, can YOU truly compete with compassion. One thing that gets lost in sports today is why we compete. A true competitor competes with himself and not just the scoreboard. Too many times people are so concerned with the result of the game, that they lose the true art of competition. What it means to be a true competitor is to have that burning desire, deep inside, that causes you to want to achieve."*

It is absolutely imperative that we help identify the "internal" and "external" motivations for participation so we can tie technical skills to behavior and attitude so the participant can recognize, maybe for the first time, why they are doing what they do. Chris addresses these points beautifully. Most players and coaches I have worked with over the years have either lost touch with the "why" of their participation or have never been in touch with it at all. That same majority loves the workshops I conduct because I help them get in touch with their "who" and "why," just like Chris did. These concepts are all learnable, no matter the stage of the athletes' or coaches' careers. Coach Gushue had coached 30 years before he met me, and Chris had grown up with the win-at-all-costs mentality. Both readily adopted the methods. More from Chris:

"Wanting to win and wanting to achieve are two separate things. Competing to win and being concerned with the final result is what eventually causes kids to give up playing sports that they once loved.

So then why do the majority of kids compete? One thing that almost always goes unnoticed is the relationships we build through competing in athletics. Thirty years from now, I probably won't remember the details of how each of those seasons went, but the things I will remember are the moments we shared together, and the bond we formed. And it's safe to say that sports are much more fun when the team is truly that, a team, rather than individuals with independent goals. Yes, you can be the most talented team, or even individual player on the field, but if you don't relish the bonds made throughout the long journey called a season, then the wins and statistics will soon be forgotten and you'll be left with nothing else to remember the season but old memories, rather than having friends for life."

Chris wanted to point out to the audience that it was the bond he formed with the entire team – starters and bench warmers – that was important. By changing where the emphasis is placed in athletics in our society, we can tap more fully into its vast potential for providing personal growth tools for all, like the spiritual nature of forming caring relationships that transcend individual accomplishments. Chris suggested that all participants can tap into the true spirit of sports by following the strategies of the Agony of Winning system.

More from Chris:

"A young athlete shouldn't judge how fun a sport is by how good he or she is at it. Despite my success on the field, I can assure you that there were guys on the team that didn't even step on the field that had just as much fun as I did. One thing we always talked about was that the accomplishments that I was achieving was not due to my ability, but rather, the work of the other guys on the practice field. We as a team set state records. And we as a team won the championship. Too much emphasis is put on personal accolades. It was great to be part of a team that stressed team accomplishments way before those of individuals and you can only hope that more young kids grow up with that mindset, but unfortunately, with the way things are going, it seems to be heading in the opposite direction. I remember this past summer I was coaching at a lacrosse camp, and we were playing a little end of the week scrimmage. The first thing the kids wanted to know was who was in charge of keeping stats. At first I thought they were joking, but soon realized that the kids really cared that

much about stats that they wanted stats kept even at a summer camp. Now yes, they were still young and not mature enough yet to totally grasp the team concept, but it's never too early to start teaching that, because the sooner they learn, the sooner they will be able to enjoy competition for all the right reasons."

When the primary emphasis and drive to compete is mostly extrinsic, winning awards and trophies, earning a scholarship, being all conference, bragging rights for the parents, and coach of the year honors, athletics ends up being a negative or losing experience for almost all who compete. What almost all parents, coaches, and players do not realize is that the extrinsic rewards and failures, for that matter, of competing are deeper, richer, and more meaningful if these experiences are in balance with intrinsic motivators. When the "what" is put into the perspective in relation to the "why" and "who," it provides tremendous power, energy, and sustainable motivation and passion for participation. The intersection of internal and external provides the foundation for a successful athletic endeavor for all participants.

It is absolutely imperative that we help identify the "internal" and "external" motivations for participation so that we can tie technical skills to behavior and attitudes so the participant can recognize, maybe for the first time, why they are doing what they do.

When **Strategy One** is incorporated, the other **Six Strategies** outlined in this book can be developed more fully because there is a commitment to the time it takes to incorporate them. The other methods will be used to emphasize the inside work the participant needs. Adopting those Strategies assures appreciation instead of the envy in the world of athletics that I observe today. It helps the individual be aware of what is going on in the process, the journey, rather than being preoccupied with the desired outcome. These strategies teach that true balance is required for the spirit of sports to remain vibrant rather than the extreme spirit-numbing nature of sports today. An end result-driven world of sports has emerged that leads to an almost frantic race to the end for all those involved. When attached to the spirit of sports, true confidence replaces the arrogance we see with so many parents, coaches, and players. Once **Strategy One** is incorporated, the following methods will help participants attach themselves to the purity of balance between external and internal motivation. In this purity, they are much more likely to be giving to the sport they are participating in instead of always taking from it. They are more likely to ask, "What can I contribute?" rather than, "What can I get out of this?" Participants competing with compassion will see that the effort the journey provides is as valuable as the end results.

I am sure you are wondering by now if you can really find relief from the Agony of Winning like Coach Gushue and Chris LaPierre did.

Isn't it a comfort to know that these easy-to-follow strategies are laid out for you page by page in this book?

Isn't it exciting to know that it is never too late to get started, no matter what stage of your coaching or playing career you are in?

The Agony of Winning workshops provided Coach Gushue and Chris with the process and they took the ball and ran with it. They scored big, and so can you.

~~~~~~

**Concept for Transforming the Agony of Winning
to the Thrill of Winning:**

*When a coach or player is aware of the "why" of their
participation, it provides the energy required when
things are not going well. In addition, the "why" provides
real goal satisfaction when things are not going well.*

~~~~~~

**Question for Transformation from Agony of Winning
to the Thrill of Winning:**

*Are parents, athletes and coaches ready to set time
aside each day to place more emphasis on the "who"
and "why" lessons?*

~~~~~~

**Word for Transforming the Agony of Winning
to the Thrill of Winning:**

Compassion

4

Why Are Sports So Important to So Many?

Athletic competition is deeply embedded in the psyche of American culture. So what is it about sports that creates such frenzy among all those involved? There is something very unique about the mind-body-spirit connection that sports can provide. The pure joy of watching or playing sports, when unencumbered by expectation and propelled by an anything-is-possible attitude, is beauty in motion. There is a unique quality inside the soul of athletic competition that is available to both the observer and the participant.

In its purest form, athletic competition appeals to the desire in all of us to strive to our highest level of excellence. There is a tremendous satisfaction, for players and coaches alike, in the intense, enthusiastic effort required to reach a desired level of success. For the observer, fans, and parents, it is exciting to witness an athlete or team challenge themselves to overcome an opponent. In addition, there are feelings of pride and joy generated internally for the observer while watching an athlete/team challenge perceived limitations and elevate themselves above what was deemed possible. These factors are at the core of our fascination with sports. This entire process provides exhilaration and excitement for the participant and observer in mostly equal doses. We are attracted to this venue like no other because of this.

Let me provide a few examples of what I am suggesting. In 1980, the U.S. hockey team, captured the hearts and minds of Americans. People like me who had no interest in hockey were excited about the possibilities of something momentous happening. Just the possibility that the team might have a chance to beat the Soviet Union, that big, bad evil empire, ignited the competitive juices inside the American people. What the U.S. hockey team did to the Soviets on the ice was almost secondary to the excitement of millions watching the drama unfold. "It's the most transcending moment in the history of our sport in this country," gushed Dave Ogrean, former executive director of USA Hockey. The transcending moment was supplied because internal satisfaction was arrived at AND the external reward, Winning, was gained. The absolute fact is that when the participants in the world of athletics embody an internal drive and passion, with the desire to accomplish external goals we a system that plays with purpose.

This leads to the next strategy of The Agony of Winning system. **Strategy Two is Competing with Purpose and Passion.**

In the 2004 Olympics in Athens, the U.S. women's soccer team upset Brazil and captured the spirit of sport for the entire nation. The manner in which they accomplished the feat touched deep into the soul of athletic competition. The players as well as observers and fans experienced the euphoria that comes with an effort to defy the odds. "I think there must have been some kind of an aura," U.S. captain Julie Foudy said. "We didn't play our best, but we gutted it out, and what better way for this team? That's what we do." Billie Jean King, the tennis legend who almost single-handedly founded the women's sports movement, said, "They are the essence of what sports are supposed to be about. They're fantastic… They have the 'it' factor. This country is indebted to them." The "it" factor is a great way to describe competing with **Purpose and Passion.** That is a powerful statement about athletic competition and how embedded it is in the American consciousness. That "it" factor refers to the internal fortitude of competing with the **Purpose and Passion** that propels an athletic team to overcome obstacles and secure the external goal, winning the GOLD MEDAL. The observer — the fans in this case — sense the energy behind the purpose and become included in the euphoric feelings that accompany being one with the team, and it's **Passion and Purpose.** Only in sports do we have this kind of energetic exchange and motivation between the participant and the observer.

There is another element that draws the athlete, parent, and coach to the intriguing energy that encompasses athletic competition. These elements are basic to humans in a general sense; however, when they are combined with the motivations I suggested in earlier paragraphs, a powerful magnetic force of high-level energy is provided. That energy is like a magnet, and it draws the masses to the wonderful world of sports. In my book "The Miracle of Optimism," I discussed some of the basic human needs that ,when filled in a positive way, provide for a joyful, high-energy, vibrant life. I think the pursuit of satisfying two of four basic human needs are what motivates so many toward sports involvement. These four essential elements are:

1. The need to be appreciated.
2. The need for consistency.
3. The need to belong to something bigger than themselves.
4. The need to experience positive personal growth in human interactions.

The two most prevalent elements found inside athletic competition are the need to be included and the need to be appreciated. Of those two, the most powerful is the need to be included.

The Agony of Winning **Strategy Two** urges participants to play and coach with ***Purpose and Passion.*** Doing so will ignite a feeling of inclusion and appreciation from parents and the fans who follow them. The following story is a perfect example of **Strategy Two** placed into action.

I have worked with the Kean University softball team, located in New Jersey, for a few seasons. I have urged them to fall in love with the spirit and essence of the game, not just the scores of the games, their statistics, or the standings. I shared with them, like I do in many of my workshops, my own story. In my life as a competitor there was always much joy present during the process of competing with my inner self;

I had a huge amount of passion for all my athletic endeavors. It always felt good when I set up little games to play, with no opponent other than my inner being. I shared with the team that as a youth I had a paper route with about 75 customers. Each day I would load my papers into a bag and place it over my left shoulder. I would take another newspaper bag and fill it with stones and hoist it over my right shoulder.

As I was delivered the papers, I would play a game where I set the rules and monitored compliance of those rules all by myself. If I was delivering on one side of the street, the object of the game was that I would take a stone from the bag and skip it across to the other side of the street, trying to hit the curb with the toss. If I hit the curb it was a win, but if I missed the curb with the rock it was a loss. It was competitive bliss. I was totally engrossed with the challenge of being able to accomplish the task at hand. I got extrinsic validation every time one of those rocks crashed into the curb. The intrinsic value of reaching for another rock with enthusiasm, **Passion and Purpose,** whether the last rock toss was a success or failure, is where the beauty of that competition shone through.

The vibrancy I felt with the energy provided by the idea that I had another chance to "win" as long as there was a rock left in the bag was indescribable, as was my connection to my own integrity — not cheating on the score, my determination in sticking with it if I had a series of missed throws, the ability to connect to the fun of trying, the fun of succeeding, the fun of missing the curb, the fun of being sure no cars were coming, the fun of connecting to the idea that competing is fun. Engaging in these types of competitions against myself provided me with the opportunity to be fully engaged with both extrinsic and intrinsic reasons for competing.

My passion and purpose for competition was evident to the Kean University softball team, and I witnessed their attachment to the idea. The team was feeling included in the story, wanting to be part of the vigor I possessed around this simple yet competitive game. I could feel their sense of appreciation for me in sharing my story with them so they could find **Purpose and Passion** in their own playing careers. The tenets of the Agony of Winning **Strategy Two** were being experienced in a very large measure by the women athletes of Kean University. As a result, much inclusion and appreciation was felt and shared throughout the program. It was a very exhilarating experience for the coaches, the players, the parents, the fans, and me. The 2008 Kean women's softball team is a shining example of **Purpose and Passion** driven athletics.

I shared my rock story with unbridled enthusiasm. I told them to always reach for another rock when things got tough, and that it's fun to get another chance to go for our goals.

The following e-mails are a compilation of messages from the team captain that reflect how they internalized the story to provide the whole team with a passionate approach to playing. In addition, the comments demonstrate inclusion and appreciation for each other and me.

Hey Coach

"... I constantly heard "win the next play, blow up the negatives and have fun." It was soo amazing I feel the spirit of the girls on my side. I am 100% convinced that we are ready to take that next rock out. We are over the losses and are looking forward from here on out.

The team is definitely playing with a Purpose and Passion.

I really appreciate the fact you followed our games today!!! They were great wins and I have to say I'm so glad that we have someone as supportive as you on our side. We actually have a surprise for you tomorrow, so we are all excited to meet with you (as we always are!)."

The team showed appreciation for the work I had done with them. They had T-shirts made for the entire team that read on the front "GOT TOUHEY," a play on the "Got Milk" commercial.

"I really enjoy the fact that more people are speaking up during our meetings now. We've come such a long way and it's great to have trust and openness on this team! Something we've been lacking through the years. Thanks to you!!!!!!"

Inclusion is demonstrated here. As a result of competing with Purpose and Passion, the entire team feels included. They feel part of the whole so feel free to share with their teammates.

"This season has been magical and the consensus is that you've been a gift from God. I've heard the girls say it many a time and I believe it. You have mentally gotten us this far and we owe it to you and ourselves to finish it the way we CAN. Thank you so much for coming to the games yesterday. You made me relax and feel at ease and truly keep in perspective that it is just a game. Your presence yesterday was a breath of fresh air."

Johanna Hedler

Senior Captain Kean University Softball Team 2008

You can see the **Passion** this team has. They have also established a **Purpose** for finishing the season strong. They owe it to themselves to do so, as Johanna writes. And they have included me and made me feel appreciated for helping them.

These e-mails represent a great example of an entire college athletic team putting **Strategy Two** put into action. Margie Akers, the Kean head softball coach who adopted **Strategy One** and allotted the time necessary to incorporate the Agony of Winning lessons garnered in **Strategy Two,** should be congratulated. She knows the game is more than bunts and home runs. She had the **Purpose and Passion** in her heart to desire more for her players, a desire that they become better people as well as better players. This is compassion-based athletics at its finest.

As radio broadcaster Paul Harvey used to say, "And now for the rest of the story." I went to see them play in the conference championships, and I sat behind a bunch of parents of the softball players. One parent took off her jacket and was wearing a T-shirt the parents had made for the playoffs. On the back of the shirt the following was printed: "Win the Next play." In other words, pick up the next rock and try to hit the curb again. It was satisfying to see how that message resonated with the players and their parents. These **Strategies** are teachable to everyone.

Sports provides the basic human need for belonging on a huge scale. The exhilaration of connecting with others on the journey toward creating desired outcomes is unmatched.

One of the 2004 Gold Medal womens' soccer players summed up the collective feeling that binds the participant and the fans with the following: "The thing I love most about this team, which I think will be the legacy, is it was always more than just soccer." He continued, "It was about giving back to fans and communities ... It's empowering to these young kids ..." That statement signifies a "we" mentality; the fan is included in the process of competing and the desired outcome.

The other primary element being satisfied in these two scenarios is that player, coach, and fans feel appreciated for their participation in the process. Human beings love that feeling. When they are appreciated for their dedication, overcoming obstacles, and sticking with the team, even if the desired outcome is not achieved, these are primary motivators for why people make sports so important.

~~~~~~~

Concept for Transforming the Agony of Winning to the Thrill of Winning:

Competing in athletics can provide the backdrop for some very basic human needs. The most important of these needs are inclusion and appreciation. Sports have the potential to satisfy these needs like no other venues. The foundation for competing with Purpose and Passion is rooted in the satisfaction of these basic human needs.

~~~~~~~

Question for Transforming the Agony of Winning to the Thrill of Winning:

What steps as a player, coach, or parent are you willing to demonstrate so those around you feel included and appreciated in the process of athletic competition?

Word for Transforming the Agony of Winning to the Thrill of Winning:

Purpose

5

Success plus Excellence

The Power of Winning

Success can be defined as attaining a favorable or desired outcome. In the world of sports today, almost all of the emphasis is on the external measurements of winning and losing, individual award acquisition, championships, being ranked No. 1, and so on. Because these external reasons/ motivators for evaluating success are so fleeting and volatile, it is difficult for most athletes to maintain a passionate approach to sports. These external methods depend almost exclusively on end results. When the sole intention of practicing and training is to assure a desirable outcome in a game or contest, what happens when that extrinsic reward is not realized? In fact, from what I am observing in sports today, even winning is being met with a muted emotional response, and the reason is that without some intrinsic value even winning is not as joyful. So what happens to the journey or process while athletes work toward the end result? Is there no value assigned to it unless the end goal is reached? Excellence in an athlete, coach, or program is incorporating goals that reflect positive character traits such as being a good teammate, having respect, contributing to the community, and most importantly, having integrity. When an athlete, coach, or team is continually striving to achieve excellence (internal satisfaction) as well as success (external satisfaction), there is tremendous power in winning.

I have worked with the talented gymnastics team at the Wilmoor School of Gymnastics, in New Jersey, owned and operated by Kevin and Kim Bonus, as well as the football teams at Cherokee High School, in New Jersey and Cornell University, located in New York. All these programs are a perfect reflection of **The Agony of Winning Strategy Three** -- to be certain that **Intrinsic** as well as **Extrinsic Goals** are being set and met.

I have been working with the Cherokee football program since 2004, and each year the program sets its **Intrinsic and Extrinsic Goals** and posts them in the locker room as a daily reminder for the players. In addition, every player signs the huge poster attached to the wall in plain view; thus, the players are committing themselves to the success and excellence of the program represented by the goals. In addition, an Agony of Winning session is held every other week during the season to talk about how the players and team are doing in relation to accomplishing their goals.

An ironic twist to this story is appropriate here. I was visiting with Al Golden, Head Football Coach at Temple University for the first time to discuss with him writing the foreword to this book. In the middle of the conversation he stopped cold and slapped his hand on the desk. I was a little startled but did not show it. He said, *"Hey, when we visited Cherokee High School last season we noticed the Intrinsic and Extrinsic Goal poster in the locker room. The players had signed the poster showing their commitment. Is that your program?"* I smiled and said, *"Yes, Coach, that poster is a result of the work I do with Coach Mehigan and the team."* Now he smiled and said, *"Well, we stole the idea. We have the same poster in our locker room signed by our players."* Then we both laughed.

I will never forget the following story. My first day in the locker room, back in 2004, I noticed an 8x11 piece of paper posted on the entrance to the locker room. There were 10 major points about what the Cherokee football program was based on. These tenets were very powerful and right on in their essence. These ten statements represented the bedrock, core concepts about what participating in the program meant. They were, however, almost exclusively extrinsic goals. For example, score this many touchdowns, hold the opponent to this many yards, win the conference, etc.

When I met for the first time with the 20 designated team leaders I asked them to name some key characteristics expected of a Cherokee football player that were listed on a piece of paper hanging in the locker room. Let's just say that although they knew the paper was posted on the bulletin board on the way into the locker room, they were unable to identify any of the statements. They really could not even tell me the essence of the core concepts of participation in the program. It should be noted that this program is full of integrity. Coach Mehigan is ahead of his time in many ways. He is a young coach who gets it about running a holistic program loaded with integrity. He was also aware that he needed some help because although the team was successful, players were suffering from the Agony of Winning. I began to get the team leaders in touch with the lofty potential of athletic participation. My goal was to deepen their attachment to the spirit of sports, beyond what already existed in the program.

So we embarked on the journey of incorporating the **Agony of Winning Strategy Three:** *Maintaining a Balance of Intrinsic and Extrinsic Goals* into a format that suited the team best. After many discussions with the leaders we developed such a system. The poster containing the core **Intrinsic and Extrinsic** goals now became the showpiece of the locker room. And just like with the Shawnee program, Temple University, Northeastern University, Kean University, Cornell University, New Egypt High School, Eastern High School, both located in New Jersey, and many others that have adopted the Agony of Winning system, there has been a culture shift within the program. The absolute fact is that when the participants in the world of athletics embody an internal drive and passion, with the desire to accomplish external goals, we have a system that plays with purpose.

Coach Mehigan dropped me this note at the end of the season:

"The Agony of Winning system taught the juniors and seniors that they needed to blend as one for the team to be successful. And just as importantly to enjoy that success. To achieve and have success with integrity. Or

excellence as you put it. We arrived at a perfect balance of internal and external goals and motivators. This was supposed to be a rebuilding year for us. Incorporating the strategies of this program certainly contradicted this in our finishing with a record of 9-2."

Strategy Three of the Agony of Winning system gets to some of the core issues that haunt athletic programs. Some of the actual intrinsic goals set by the Cherokee teams over the years are *Enjoyment and Relaxation, Friendship and Relationships, Playing with a Sense of Purpose and Passion, Appreciate One Another, A Basic Love of Competition, Have a Lot of Fun, and Feel Part of Something.* This is not the normal locker room motivation material that gets posted. However, it is real and has substance.

The beautiful thing about the Agony of Winning system is that when properly implemented, it leads the coaches and players down the path of competing with compassion. For example, one year there were two players who had been friends and played ball together for many years. It just so happened that they both liked the same girl. These were two important players in terms of the impact this circumstance could have on the team's extrinsic goals. One of the stated goals was to win a state championship. At one of our sessions, some of the players said they could feel the tension between these two players on the practice field and it was having a negative effect on team morale.

The leaders were basically sharing that the **Intrinsic** goal of achieving solid *Friendship and Relationships* within the team was being compromised by these two players' strained friendship. I asked the two players to come to the front of the room and sit and face each other and talk about this incident.

They both shared honestly and openly with each other and agreed that what was happening was hurting the team and their friendship. The rest of the team then shared how the strained relationship was affecting them. Both players apologized to each other, the team, and the program and agreed to put it behind them and move on. The Agony of Winning was being played out in that room full of team leaders. That Agony was also noticeably alleviated right in front of my eyes. The power of the Agony of Winning system is immense.

Another experience I had with the Cherokee team, in another season, also had to do with their **Intrinsic** goals, that particular goal being to *appreciate one another.* One of the players on the 2004 team, Jeff Maccarella, wrote me the following e-mail.

> *"First off, thank you for all that you done thus far with our team. It (meaning the Agony of Winning system) is already working with the team. I'm very, very thankful for this opportunity that you have provided me with. Our last meeting was really an eye-opener to me; it made me realize a lot about myself, not just as a football player but as a person. I don't know if we can do it this Thursday, but maybe we can tell each other how much we really appreciate each other. Have every person in the room say something to someone else. I was talking with the guys after the last meeting and it hit me that this exercise would be great for everyone in the room."*

This e-mail was sent by an 18-year-old talented football player. I mention that because many adults in athletics assume this kind of intimacy is beyond what teenagers are capable of. I guess not. This team experienced less of the Agony of Winning because of exercises like this one. I incorporated this particular appreciation exercise into the system and have used it since.

One of the more powerful scenarios regarding the appreciating exercise was experienced with the Cornell University football team. About 75 players and the entire staff attended my session at summer football camp. The coaches participated and chose another coach to whom they would read their appreciation list. It was amazing to watch the players observe the exchange between one of the assistants and the head coach, Jim Knowles. So as the assistant coach read the first line to Coach Knowles, this big, tough defensive assistant began to cry. The level of emotion and appreciation expressed about the integrity of the head coach was amazing to witness. The assistant coach expressed tremendous love and gratitude for Coach Knowles. The whole team enjoyed the feeling of appreciation as they observed the exchange between the two men. The power in the room was astounding. The energy level was through the roof. I think it was especially powerful for these young men to see their head coach with a tear trickling down his check. They were able to see his more human side and felt closer to him. They became even more committed to working hard for him and the Cornell program. The team now had a stronger bond. Coach Jim Knowles wrote me the following note: *"You are to heart related performance enhancement what Bill Walsh was to the West Coast Offense when he was with the 49ers. People will seek you out in droves to implement your system."*

I will never forget using this exercise with the high-level gymnasts at the Wilmoor School of Gymnastics. The gym's owner Kim Bonus, hired me because she wanted to demonstrate to the gymnasts' parents that a holistic approach to the sport was necessary. In one of our sessions, I asked the girls to write three things they appreciated about one of their teammates. The girls of Wilmoor had plenty of **Extrinsic goals**. Each one of the 12 athletes I was working with were college scholarship-level athletes. They listed as **Extrinsic** goals routine high score goals, winning meet goals, and being the best in the gym goals, but not many **Intrinsic** goals. I was able to establish with them that the real power behind those **Extrinsic** goals would be magnified and more satisfying when accomplished if they married them to some **Intrinsic** goals. Once we established the **Intrinsic** goals, they all listed appreciation for one another as one of their primary goals. During a workshop, I had each gymnast stand face to face with a teammate for whom they had written an appreciation statement. Then they read the following simple statements to their fellow gymnasts: *"What I appreciate about you most is___."* They each repeated that simple line three times, filling in the blank with a different quality that they appreciated about the other. It was powerful, and every one of the top-notch athletes cried while they watched their teammates feel appreciated.

Emily Santoro was one of the athletes who benefited the most by hearing how much her fellow gymnasts appreciated her. It enhanced her performance beyond her wildest dreams. The Agony of Winning system helped Emily be more compassionate with herself as she competed. When others showed their appreciation, she internalized her own abilities and believed anything was possible for her. And it was. The following are e-mails that Emily's mother sent to Kim Bonus and I after Emily went off to college and became a champion college gymnast. The first one was sent after I had a brief session on the phone with Emily to reminder her of her talents and let her know that sustaining the energy to be a champion required **Intrinsic** goals in addition to her **Extrinsic** goal of being the best gymnast at Cornell University.

Hi Kevin,

Thank you, thank you, and thank you!!!!!!!!!!!!!!

She had a great meet! Third on floor with a 9.8! She had looked more at peace than when I saw her prior to her speaking with you. You are amazing.

Thank you again,

Stephanie

I love the fact that her mother points out that Emily seemed at peace. That is awesome. An in-the-zone athlete is at peace when they compete. That is because they have married **Intrinsic** and **Extrinsic** goals.

After the season, Kim and I received the following e-mail of appreciation from Stephanie Santoro:

Good Morning!!

This may be a long synopsis, but I wouldn't know how to really shorten it. In the end this would not have been possible for Emily without all your help and support! Kim, I'll never forget what you asked me when Em first came to Willmoor, "What do you want for Emily?" I replied that she would be happy. With all your guidance she was not only happy, but at peace and it all came through. She fell on both events at prelims, but pulled it together with all you taught her and nailed it when they truly needed it!

So Em is a National Champ and Cornell did it without any athletic scholarship and they were the team that tied both nights!

My thanks, much gratitude and love to you Kim and Kevin!

Love,

Stephanie

When the delivery system for athletic competition marries **Intrinsic** motivators for competing with **Extrinsic** reasons, we arrive at a more passionate approach to the games we play. This **Strategy** employs a system that will provide a powerful moment-to-moment engagement to the task at hand. When all those involved with athletics -- parents, athletes, and coaches -- are engaged with compassion-based athletics, they understand that the reasons for their participation lie not only in the striving for outward measurements of success but intrinsically as well. They are fully aware of whether they are achieving excellence, this measurement inside them.

The true end result will be a more passionate approach to sports. The participant will become aware of the true purpose of athletic competition because they will have applied the "why" and the "who" of their participation to the "what" of their participation, maybe rediscovering the lost spirit of sports or perhaps discovering it for the first time.

Concept for Transforming the Agony of Winning to the Thrill of Winning:

It is imperative that coaches, parents, and athletes take a hard look at their internal motivations for participation in athletics. All the energy and power reside in setting **Intrinsic** *goals to coincide with* **Extrinsic** *goals.*

Question for Transforming the Agony of Winning to the Thrill of Winning:

What are your top five reasons for participation in athletics? Are they internal or external? Is there a balance between the two?

Word for Transforming the Agony of Winning to the Thrill of Winning:

Motivation

6

Parental Paranoia in the New Age of Sports

"Once you put up the score boards and standings and all those things parents think it's the Flyers, the Eagles, and the Phillies (three of the areas pro teams). They don't realize there are volunteer parents out there coaching their children," says Fred Engh, president of the National Alliance for Youth Sports. So many coaches, parents, and players that I have witnessed over the years have seen the spirit and passion of their participation suffer under the burden of expectation. Parents need to take a hard look at what they are subjecting their children and volunteer coaches to in the youth leagues across America.

The Agony of Winning **Strategies Two and Three** -- to have purpose and passion while competing and being sure to set intrinsic as well as extrinsic goals -- are truly highlighted throughout this chapter.

In the era in which I played, parental involvement was limited to the adult volunteers coaching the team. In other words, there were no parents hovering around practice and games so close you could feel them, except my dad. He was way ahead of his time – a role model, if you will, for the modern parent. It amazes me that parents of youth league players set up around the field and courts as if it were a tailgate party, to watch practice. I often wondered why they didn't have something else more interesting to do. I am grateful that my father was ahead of his time, but at least he did not come and watch practice like the parents of this era. However, he was a human athletic pressure cooker and he provided me with the perspective for what I am observing today in other parents.

Because of the way I experienced sports as a youngster, I can see very clearly where the "beauty and the beast" of athletics resides. Some personal history is appropriate here. As I have already described, my earliest attachment to sports was pure and healthy. Fun, if you will! But as I said I was born to compete, and as I began to do so things changed. I think my dad was looked at as kind of an intense person who was always on the refs, or yelling at the coach. Nothing ever pleased him. In the 1960's and '70s he was outside the norm. Today, I think he would fit right in -- there is such intensity around success from the media, parents, and coaches that I think playing sports is stressful for a majority who play. It is very difficult for me to even go to a game because of the immediate negative reactions of almost everyone in the stands.

I live outside Philadelphia, and there are pro teams for all the major sports. There is ample opportunity to watch pro sports, with pros and cons to that situation. I think the expectation from the parents for high-level performance trickles down from the pro level to the youngest of athletes. The youth leagues become a mini version of the big guys, right down to the full uniforms and rah-rah cheerleaders.

I mentioned Fred Barnett, a friend of mine, in a previous chapter. He has twin daughters the same age as my daughter Serena, 9. Fred Barnett is a former NFL All-Pro receiver who played most of his career with the Philadelphia Eagles. In addition, he spent some time with the Miami Dolphins. Fred enjoyed a quality NFL career and was a panelist on the Agony of Winning forum. During his talk he continually asked the parents and coaches in the audience, "What are we doing to our young athletes? What is the purpose? What are the adults doing to their passion for competing? What internal goals are we helping them set so they know it is about more than just trophies and awards?" These are great questions, and Fred was not even aware he was asking them about **Strategies Two and Three** from the Agony of Winning system. He was asking, however, for all those involved to begin to implement a more compassion-based system for competition.

He wrote this piece to be included in this book and I am grateful:

> *"When I see the way parents and coaches are approaching the sports experience with kids, I see a crash in the near future; I picture physical, emotional, and psychological devastation. I see resentment from the kids, hatred for the organized sport, which is intended*

to be just an activity or a platform to teach our young girls and boys all the wonderful characteristics and important lessons of life. The bar for parental pressure has not been raised too high on the lengths parents are going to assure "success" for their children, compared to past generations of athletes, because the bar does not exist! There are no limits!

Once again Fred is asking, "What is the purpose? Where are the Intrinsic Goals? Where is the dedication in youth sports to teaching the Life Lessons?"

He continued on:

It should only be a fantasy for a 12 year old to dream about being a professional baseball player. Unfortunately, coaches and parents are trying to make the thought a reality at such a young age in the modern era of youth sports. With the parents' reality drilled into their minds, the arms will go out for the young pitchers, the shoulders for the young swimmers, the knees for the young gymnasts, the head trauma for the young running backs and linebackers will continue to be the real truth of their children's participation... Most importantly, their passion for playing, their spirit will be diminished and will go out the window under all the pressure from parents...The spirit to enjoy the experience of competition will fade slowly. In real time, it's becoming a loss when your kids win. By no means should a pre teen have the stress of winning or losing a game. The Agony of Winning is a sad but true statement for our young people today and it shouldn't be in our vocabulary."

However, what eventually happened to my dad happens to others, which is that the extrinsic goal of achieving No. 1 and winning becomes an obsession and the only thing that matters to most everyone involved with sports. That obsession is fueled by the media – more about that later. Playing, making it fun, learning from the experience, and growing as a person has become secondary in today's world of athletics. Today a whole nation of athletes and families of athletes are chasing a result from competition that is a myth. That myth? That winning is the only reward in competition.

In many ways the media has provided parents with a tremendous amount of information. It is often said that parents are much more knowledgeable today than in eras gone by. There is another saying that knowledge in the wrong hands can be dangerous. Parents think they know more. I have found them no more knowledgeable now than when I was coaching 25 years ago. They are simply armed with a whole lot more "sound bite" information that has given them a feeling of entitlement like at no other time.

Parents empowered by the constant "sound bite" analysis in the media believe they have attained a status equal to the coach's. They are under the false impression that their opinions are the truth and as valid as those of the coach trained in the children's sports. In a high school sports blog, Bob Behre writes, "In case you didn't notice, parents know everything about sports their kids are playing. It is truly uncanny how these know-it-alls have figured it all out while holding down a full time job." I love the truth revealed in that statement. There is such a small margin of error for coaches in the insane, sports-crazed culture that exists today.

In the past 20 years the negative energy level of parents has multiplied in an alarming fashion, so much so that some youth leagues are banning parents from games. Where is all this anger and frustration coming from? I think one of the biggest factors is the parent trying to vicariously attain some level of accomplishment for themselves through their children. On an even deeper level, I think parents are looking to increase their own self-esteem through their children's achievements. This is very dangerous. A third reason is the fact that so many adults live unsatisfactory lives in terms of their work that they are pursuing some fulfillment from their children's athletic careers. This is a tremendous burden for a student/athlete to carry onto the ice, courts, or playing fields of competition.

I see parents express a lot of frustration at sporting events, whether it is anger over the coaching, the referees, other people's children, or their own child. I resent that they are able to spout all that negativity all over the bleachers just because they have assumed some sort of entitlement. I have often told coaches and athletes in my performance and leadership workshops that it would be cool if we could set up some bleachers in their parents' workplaces. I teach them that as athletic performers in the modern era, they are under uncommon scrutiny and evaluation from those watching them, particularly parents. I tell them to picture, for instance, that they are at their parent's real estate office and fans are allowed to watch the parent perform. The bleachers are full. The band is playing, and the cheerleaders are leading everyone in a cheer – "GET THAT SALE, GET THAT SALE!!" In the heat of battle as the parent is trying to close the deal, it a pivotal point, it is win or lose.

The parent decides to employ a tactic to close the sale, one they learned though a vigorous set of course work they were required to take to become a licensed, professional salesperson. The plumber, accountants, math teacher, store clerk, and college president, all in attendance to watch the contest, and who know nothing about real estate sales strategy, disagree with the tactic used by the salesperson. They all begin to yell at the real estate professional. "What in the heck were you thinking about going for that bone-headed close to the sales deal? What are you, stupid?" I ask my workshop attendees, "How do you think that parent would feel?" I would love to see that scene, just once, and would joyfully pay the admission fee.

The "Courier-Post," the largest newspaper in South Jersey, asked young athletes to write in with a response to the following topic: Parents and Sports. The question was the following: *What should be done to prevent overly aggressive parents from doing harm to athletes, referees and other parents during youth games?"*

Here are a few of the responses.

"Well, you don't have to look any further than the sidelines filled with eager parents. You see, parents believe they can get away with almost anything at a sports event. For some weird reason, parents think a bad call gives them the right to yell, scream, and throw temper tantrums that would rival that of a two-year-old."

Rob Cooper, Senior at Williamsburg High School, Williamsburg, PA

"Too often, the parent fails to realize that embarrass-ment, due to violent actions and/or negative remarks such as 'you could have made that shot, what's wrong with you!' can hurt severely. It is crucial that parents consistently encourage their young athletes by making a positive contribution during the sports season."

Teneke Bailey, Senior at Highpoint High School, Highpoint, NJ

~~~~~~~~~

"It's a sick world that we live in when overly aggressive parents can't keep their insults to themselves in sporting events. Whether they're offending a referee over a call, affronting another parent for some foolish reason, or giving the children a hard time while they're playing, unstable parents disrupt the games and take the fun out of athletics for their children. I've learned from witnessing exceedingly insistent parents that their yelling never accomplishes anything positive. When they give the kids a hard time, the child will most likely play worse because he/she will falter under the harsh pressure. Arguing with other parents over their youngsters' game is simply foolish. This is a youth level sport."

Colleen Salemi, 8th-grader at Olson Middle School

These young people have a very good perspective on the out of control behavior of parents. It is time for this to stop. The time has come for parents to take a good hard look at their own "why" and "who." It is also time they hold themselves accountable and get a grip on their motivations and behaviors.

The **Agony of Winning Strategies** hold some promise for this situation. For instance, competing with **Passion and Purpose** has an application that Fred Barnett and I presented in our forum for fans and parents. These very teachable strategies may just provide the skills necessary to observe competition in a whole new way.

Barnett provided a powerful vignette during his presentation that night for all the parents of young athletes. He said:

> *"I have twin daughters who are 9 years old and they free swim. Free swim doesn't mean my wallet is not damaged for them being able to use the pool. It means that they are not damaged as they compete within the class and learn the different techniques of swimming. Oh, they learn the Intrinsic based lessons of how to be dedicated and consistent in order to get it right, Kevin talks about these important lessons in the Agony of Winning Strategies.*
>
> *Interestingly, they were on sports teams. They were actually good. Maybe because their father was a pro football player or their mother was a long time dancer. However, the even more interesting part of this story is that they are not in organized sports now. Why? I'm proud to say it was their choice, and what valid choices they were. Myla, at 8 years old, an A student, and all the evidence of being a great gymnast, placed 1st and two 2nd's in the YMCA Nationals, with only a year of coaching. She started to fall behind in class work. In addition, in her social life, because of her commitment*

to the gym, she would have to miss the birthday parties of her friends because of her competitions. She was not having it! Projects being late for school and missing the experience with her friends out of the class room was not an option for her, not at 8 years old. I had no problem with it. Yes! I see all the potential in the world in her effort but her efforts belong to her experience and her experience belongs to her life, not mine!

Hailey, who was 8 years old at the time, truly runs like the wind, never gets tired. She loved track practice. She often smiled after winning the practice runs as all the adults would frown and marvel at the distance she would win by. She knew all the parents and the coaches and thought that running was a great experience. Her first meet, the stands are full, new faces, people she doesn't know, she decided not to run because it was too much pressure on her. It was too much for HER, not the other kids. That day she won because she understood what she could handle, I also won as a father for preparing her to communicate when the fears of her heart spoke to her and to listen to them."

I know there were parents in the audience who almost fell off their chairs when Barnett told this story. There were parents who told me in the days following the forum that Barnett was teaching his kids to be quitters. I told those parents that his children were only 8 years old. He was really teaching them great decision-making skills and demonstrated great empathic listening skills. These are compassion-based skills that his children are learning with their participation in athletics as the classroom. These are intrinsic lessons rooted in the heart. The parents in the audience got to see a view that makes sense.

Perhaps as a result of hearing Barnett's story, parents may see the intrinsic virtues of sports as well as pushing their children to achieve external success. When we can train the parents in the Agony of Winning principles, they will become less attached to the end results, the outcome of the athletic experience. They may tap into their responsibility for recognizing the holistic value of competition and the importance of what is occurring during the journey that they can learn from. Just like Barnett and his children learned from their journey.

If we are able to do this with youth programs, the message of the Agony of Winning will make its way to the high school, college, and even the pro levels.

With the tenets of the Agony of Winning Strategies fully established for parents and observers, perhaps they will be aware that the true essence of sports is a balance of intrinsic and extrinsic goals. This will enable them to cheer their team or individual on to winning passionately, while remaining civil. They may be appreciative, instead of envious of the opponents and other members of their own team. While cheering vigorously for their side to beat the other side, they may be able to value the quality of the effort, not just the end result. They may realize that paying attention to the full spectrum of what playing with a purpose means may become a less stressful experience for all. The end result then turns into something very different, knowledge of the ongoing spiritual truth of participation in sports, that it provides all its participants the chance to become better people.

When parents learn compassion-based athletics while they are in the process of enrolling their children in one-on-

one training sessions, traveling to swimming meets, to AAU games, spending countless dollars on gymnastics fees and summer camps, they will be expecting a different outcome. Parents would understand that a portion of the time, energy, and money that they were expending was being used to enhance intrinsic excellence, as well as extrinsic skill development. When there is commitment to the intrinsic value of sports there would be less emphasis on "what" level of extrinsic success is. The parents will not be so intent on asking themselves the following question: "What is this commitment of time and money going to buy my child?"

Of course, the coaches and players focusing on intrinsic values would also be invested in striving for internal excellence as well as external success. If the ability to perform a better breast stroke could be perfected while the athlete and coach were engaged with equal vigor in providing an opportunity for personal growth, we would have the foundation for passionate, purposeful athletic participation. If everyone involved knew that character education, good sportsmanship, and leadership skills, coupled with humility and grace, were as important as the end result of winning, we would have a system that competes with compassion and less stress. Thus, we are providing a transformation process away from the Agony and toward the Thrill.

The Thrill of Winning is more accessible to coaches and players who realize that the balance of intrinsic and extrinsic motivators is the key. Excellence is arrived at when there is a high level of positive energy applied to the task at hand, in the present moment. Passion is created by the moment-to-moment enthusiastic engagement in practice and training with an eye on mastering the extrinsic goals. It really boils down to each individual becoming the best self they can become on their way to achieving honorable extrinsic goals and satisfaction.

I think the essence of what excellence means is best summed up by legendary UCLA Hall of Fame basketball coach John Wooden. He said, "My prescription for success is based on something my father used to tell me. You should never try to be better than someone else, but you should never cease trying to be the best you can be." This statement is at the core of arriving at success (extrinsic) through the method of being excellent (intrinsic). What he is saying is that when you realize there is no opponent but yourself, you are competing with something inside yourself. It would do parents, players and coaches a lot of good to adhere to this philosophy. I can tell you from personal experience this is a powerful way to prepare, not just for athletic contests, but for the game of life as well.

~~~~~~~~

Concept for Transforming the Agony of Winning to the Thrill of Winning:

When a coach or player is aware of the "why" of their participation it provides real goal satisfaction when things are going well.

~~~~~~~~

Question for Transforming the Agony of Winning to the Thrill of Winning:

What is the most important aspect of participation in athletics? Winning games? Having fun? Learning life lessons? Whether you are a parent, coach, or player, where are you placing the most emphasis? Is your perspective balanced?

~~~~~~~~

Word for Transforming the Agony of Winning to the Thrill of Winning:

Fun

7

The Agony of Winning

Athletic Code of Ethics

While I was writing this chapter a client of mine called in tears. This was a coach who had hired me to work with his team to relieve the Agony of Winning that was widespread among the players and parents in his program. He made a commitment, both financial and of his time, to have me work with the team to establish a set of values upon which to base their athletic participation. He had a good team and was certain it would be successful in terms of winning games. However, he also thought it was important that the players be aware of why they were playing and who they were while winning. The coach knew the team needed **Strategy One: Agony of Winning Triangle: The "Who," "What," and "Why" of Athletics.** His assessment was right on.

The first day I met with the team I faced a talented group of players who were going to win a lot of games. I also faced a team with zero – and I mean zero – passion left for the game. I knew it was going to take a heavy dose of the **Agony of Winning Strategy Two: Competing with Purpose and Passion**, to bring this team back to life.

I began to conduct workshops with the team, coaches, and parents. The coach adopted the 7 Strategies with full force and wanted the entire basketball community on the same page with his philosophy. Its roots were deep in the principles of the Agony of Winning. He committed the time needed to work on the more spirit-based messages that athletic competition can potentially teach. One of the tenets he stressed was the integrity of the athletes' relationships with each other, the coaches, and the fans who followed the team. Its members went on to win many games – actually, a few more than expected – and the overall positive energy the athletes derived from each other served them well. When players lost a few tough games they were able to rely on the lessons they learned from **Strategy Two: Competing with Purpose and Passion.** The "why" and the "who" of their participation carried them through the tough stretch so the principles they derived from **Strategy One: Agony of Winning Triangle: The "Who," "What," and "Why" of Athletics** was the foundation they relied on to get back on track.

The coach sent me this e-mail testimony after the season,

"We had a group of girls who were burned out from basketball. They had no feelings either way pertaining to their experience of being part of the team. Through your workshop, Kevin, you helped the girls draw their own conclusion as to what was really important about competing and being part of the team. Things like appreciating one another, supporting one another, building character and having an impact on making a difference in each other's lives.

It was amazing to witness how quickly the passion and excitement to compete came back to these passionless girls. The love and appreciation they had for each other was at a whole different level. The games and practices became fun again. Kevin, you taught us all that we spend too much time on concentrating on the outcome or end result, and not enough time enjoying the little experiences and lessons along the way. The end result was that these kids loved being with each other. They became fierce competitors who would run through a brick wall for each other. We did not become soft; we became powerful. The girls enjoyed a very successful season with an incredible win-loss record. In addition, we became district champions and regional finalists."

The coach understood it was important for the parents to be on board with the philosophy he was putting into place with the team. He felt it was important that he include them and show them his appreciation for the privilege of coaching their daughters. He asked me to conduct a workshop for the parents and required that they attend. It fascinates me how much parents struggle with the concept that athletics has so much more to offer their children than the end results of score of the games and scholarship attainment. They have invested so much time, money, and travel in making their children better players that helping them become better people through their participation has become secondary. Nonetheless, this coach wanted the parents exposed to **Strategy *One: Agony of Winning Triangle*** so he asked me to conduct a parent workshop. At least one of the parents missed the point of the workshop.

The coach called in tears because the administration of the school had informed him that the family of one of his players, including the player, had filed a formal complaint of emotional abuse against him. He was being put on notice that his own behaviors toward the player were being investigated and that he might not be retained as head basketball coach. In reality, the parents were upset because their child had been the star player of the team, under a different coach, her first three years of high school. The new coach preached a more balanced team approach that did not feature just one player. This was not satisfactory to the parents despite the success of this new team philosophy in terms of wins and losses.

It did not matter to the parents that everyone was contributing and the team spirit and moral were at an all-time high. It mattered little to these parents that the energy of the team ignited the inclusionary needs of the entire student body, which was following the team in an unprecedented fashion. The entire school had found the principles of the **Agony of Winning Strategy Two: *Competing with Purpose and Passion,*** and the whole school was experiencing the Thrill of Winning. However, these parents had a long, miserable season because their daughter was no longer the queen of the court. Why? Because they had invested so much time, money, and travel so their child could attain an athletic scholarship and this new coach was interfering with that. They saw their opportunity going down the drain against the holistic approach that was producing team unity, spirited play, inspirational team energy, and the shared responsibility of the entire team to ensure the implementation of *Strategy Three: Maintaining a Balance of Intrinsic and Extrinsic Goals.* These truths about the program were not enough to please these selfish parents. It follows the logic of a selfish parent with only one concern – WHAT CAN I GET OUT OF THIS FOR MY DAUGHTER? – that they would seek revenge against the coach.

I guess what really set the parents off was the fact that their child had revealed to them that there would be no college career; she was quitting the sport after high school. The player decided a great high school career was sufficient and she was not going to compete on the college level. She decided she simply wanted to experience college as a student. The coach had known their daughter since she was in the fourth grade. In fact, this man had been her coach in the summer leagues all of her playing career before high school. He did not care that the parents were upset with him. However, he could not contain himself as he told me the player had also signed the complaint. He could not believe she really felt that way about him. In his heart and mind he had done all he could to show her there is more to the game than its outcome and a college scholarship. He thought the lessons of civility, respect, empathy, integrity, and compassion were important to her growth as a person. The coach also believed those lessons had been taught successfully.

The coach was sure that **Strategy Four: The Agony of Winning Code of Ethics: Setting a Tone for Integrity, Respect, and Civility** had a foothold within his program. He especially had me emphasize the **Integrity** element of the code for the players. We spent a lot of time in the sessions teaching the players and coaches what **Integrity** meant and how important it is to apply it to everyday life.

I call **Integrity** the "Looking in the Mirror" ethic. Living life with integrity means you can look in the mirror each and every night, content that you have kept your word to the very best of your ability. First of all, you are alone when you are looking in the mirror; no one is checking up on you to hold you accountable. So you are being honest with yourself when no one is watching. While looking in the mirror you will be able to hold yourself accountable for the choices you made during that 24-hour period. Did you do what was right and truthful or did you take some short cuts out of **Integrity** that were simply more convenient?

Before you glance away from your reflection in the mirror, did this revealing exercise allow you to say, "I did the right thing today even though it might have worked to my disadvantage on a few occasions?" It is important to tell yourself the truth. As John Wooden said, "Tell the truth. That way you don't have to remember a story." Be honest while looking in the mirror. In the final analysis it is always between YOU and YOU. No one else. **Integrity** means you have trained yourself to live up to what you say you are, to act or behave in accordance with the truth about yourself, and to hold yourself accountable when you fall short of that. There is a certain peace and serenity that accompanies living in **Integrity**. That is because you are living a spiritual universal truth. I think what hurt the coach the most is he thought the player had become a model for **Strategy Four: The Agony of Winning Code of Ethics: Setting a Tone for Integrity, Respect, and Civility.** He sent me an e-mail and here is an excerpt that reflects his belief that the players had adopted the tenet of having a high level of integrity:

> *"The benefit we all experienced was that we all became better people and demonstrated more character. We also learned how precious the experience of building relationships that are meaningful within the team can be such a powerful force."*

However, **Integrity** does not mean not making a mistake or an error in judgment. It means correcting it when you do. This player took just 24 hours to realize she was out of **Integrity**. I cannot be certain, but I can almost see this student/athlete looking in the mirror and deciding that she did not like the way being out of **Integrity** felt and she did not like what was looking back at her. Perhaps she recalled our session in which the players and coaches were asked to pick out a person in the room and write what they appreciated about them. Maybe when she looked in the mirror, the face of the person she chose was who she saw looking back at her. Just maybe she remembered she had chosen the coach as the person she most respected and appreciated.

In the team workshop when I asked the group to share whom they had chosen and why, this player was one of the first ones to share. She readily shared with her teammates and coaches how much she admired and looked up to the head coach for the manner in which he cared about his players. She shared all the valuable lessons he had taught her. There is no question in my mind that her parents put her up to striking out at the coach, especially after she decided not to play college ball. However, to her credit, her own **Integrity** won in the end. She went back to the administration the next day and recanted. She was crying as she told the administration that what she and her parents had said the day before about the coach was not true. It took great courage for this player to go against her parents' wishes. They seemed not to understand that in their daughter's experiences in sports, the most valuable principle was the universal truth of **Respect** and **Integrity**. In the end she valued her spiritual relationship with the coach.

There is a tremendous need in the world of sports to set a new tone of **Respect, Integrity, and Civility**. In sports culture today, as I have discussed in preceding chapters, a very negative tone in relationships has been accepted as normal. The norm today is this general tone of incivility and it is universal within all elements of athletic competition from administration right down to youth coaches. Subsequently, I am advocating the adoption of a **Strategy Four: The Agony of Winning Code of Ethics: Setting a Tone for Integrity, Respect, and Civility** for players, media, parents, fans, and coaches.

This **Strategy** addresses the "who" part of the **Agony of Winning Triangle**. If all those involved in athletics lived by this code, their observable actions and demonstrated behavior would be increasingly civil and less stressful. I believe negativity is like a virus, a very contagious virus. I know feelings and emotions are a breeding ground for the growth of this virus. In its grown-up form these negative feelings bloom into a stress-filled environment simply because the overall tone is one of negativity. It is incredibly difficult, almost impossible, to have any fun in a stress-laden athletic culture. This stress has worked its way down from the professional ranks to the youngest athletes. **A Code of Ethics** will provide the antidote to the virus. A dose of **Integrity, Respect, and Civility** are just what the doctor ordered.

It is my contention that in the last 20 years ethical compliance has taken a big spiral downwards. What do I mean by ethics in athletics? How do they apply to a cast of players, sports media, coaches, and parents/fans? I can already hear the howls from the most ferocious competitors saying, "Here we go again with the Agony of Winning and competing with compassion," They may refer to it as the Oprah Factor, the "sissafacation" of the American athlete. The implementation of **Strategy Four: The Agony of Winning Code of Ethics: Setting a Tone for Integrity, Respect, and Civility** will certainly change the face of athletes as we know it, but not to something less competitive. However, it is important that we let go of the "winning at all cost" attitude, regardless of what that takes. The fact is athletes often become the leaders of tomorrow in business, education, and government. What kind of leadership do we want? We want leaders to be of high integrity, do we not? Athletics holds the key to an educational system that provides a balance between ensuring victories in the contests that are played and winning in life for all the participants. Winning the games in sports and in life with respect, with honor, with integrity, and with a civil tone is important. That is compassion-based athletics. The Agony of Winning **Strategy Four** teaches those elements for application by parents, coaches, and players during the competition process.

In the media, in this case "Sports Illustrated," I came across an article written by Dan Patrick. Dan was interviewing Danica Patrick (no relation) and he asked if she would take performance-enhancing drugs if she would not get caught and it would lead to her winning the Indianapolis 500. Her answer to this question, which was published for thousands of young athletes to read, is priceless. There is an indelible line that can be drawn between her statement and others like it to the fact that we have reduced the **Integrity** of sports to a new low. Danica's response:

> *"Well, then it's not cheating, is it? If nobody finds out? Yeah, it would be like finding a gray area. In motorsports, we work in gray areas a lot. You're trying to find where the holes are in the rule book."*

Beautifully put, Danica, that theory is filtering its way down to the youth of America in a big way. You can count on it.

Concept for Transforming the Agony of Winning to the Thrill of Winning:

*It is vitally important that players, coaches, and parents realize they are all on the same team. All three segments need to understand that the **Integrity** of the athletic experience is rooted in maintaining a respectful, civil approach to one another.*

Question for Transforming the Agony of Winning to the Thrill of Winning:

Do you recall an incident when you acted in a way that was out of alignment with your own Integrity? How would you amend those thoughts or actions if you could?

Word for Transforming the Agony of Winning to the Thrill of Winning:

Understanding

8

The Agony of Winning

Responsible Leadership

One of the benefits of incorporating **Strategy Four: The Agony of Winning Code of Ethics: Setting a Tone for Integrity, Respect, and Civility** into athletic programs is that we will be training future leaders to have an ethical motivation and responsibility to do the right thing. A code of ethics is about having an overriding desire to do what is right. **Integrity** beckons us to practice self-restraint. You do not change your ethics on a whim or under certain circumstances. You also do not alter your ethics as situations change. Ethics are a constant and guide your decision making and actions regardless of condition or circumstances. There is an **Intrinsic** nature to ethics. Demonstrating a commitment to ethical practices in athletics is **"who"** you are being in your interactions with others and your relation to the competition itself. Your actions are observable and reflective of the value system of the parents, coaches, and players. In other words, the **"why" of** their participation. Ethics must become the foundation upon which we build our value system. What I mean is that the universal truth of **Integrity, Civility, and Respect** is the basic foundation of a values-based athletic experience. There are many shining examples of the application of the principals of **Strategy Four** in the world of sports. I know that this is a teachable **Strategy**. I know that if athletic programs, as a whole, adopted **Strategy One** and alloted the time needed to employ all the **Strategies of the Agony of Winning,** everyone involved would benefit. The end result will be a transformational process from the Agony of Winning back to the Thrill of Winning.

Let me share a shining example from the college level that drives this point home. Former St. John Fisher baseball Coach Dan Pepicelli modeled ethics and values in a huge way with his team. During one of the team's games, a hard liner hit down the third base line struck the other team's coach. He slumped to the ground unconscious. For years Pepicelli made his team sit down before the season and talk about their values, about ethics, and about how they could be implemented on the field of play, as well as the larger applications in their lives outside of athletic competition. In this particular year the team talked about honesty, hard work, loyalty, respect, success, and family. Pepicelli stated, "That last one was my favorite." He also wanted to be sure that his team was accountable to those values and that their behavior demonstrated a practical application of their stated ethics and values. In other words, Coach Pepicelli was challenging his team to be "who" they said they were going to be while they played and competed. He wanted them to be clear that they had an ethical commitment in their actions. To Coach Pepicelli, the entire baseball community was family, not just the members of his own team.

When the opposing coach was hit, a member of the "baseball" family, the larger whole, the entire extended family of the baseball community, was "hit" with the ball. So when Oswego coach Frank Paini was struck in the head, Coach Pepicelli knew that what he and his team did next would speak volumes about their ethics and values. He rushed to Paini's side to see if he could be of any assistance. Then he went to the dugout to consult with his team. They decided the only thing they could do was to stop playing, and concede the game, which ended the playing career of his senior players. He thought it best to model that the score and outcome of the game were secondary to the health of the opposing coach – a member of the baseball family – and the **Integrity** of his team living up to their ethics and values. Coach Pepicelli was recently hired as the pitching coach at Clemson University. I think he picked a good program, and Clemson chose the right coach. Clemson Head Coach Jack Leggett said, *"Getting the guys to buy into doing the right thing all the time is very important."* Now that is ethical behavior and a powerful message from the coach that shows tremendous leadership. It also speaks to the fact that the Agony of Winning **Strategies** are teachable and can be applied on all levels of competition. Clemson University now has two coaches who believe in their responsibility of training ethical leaders.

Conversely, there are many instances that show the athletic world that there is much work to be done in establishing a system where the outcome of games is not the most important thing. The journey or process of how we get there is more important. If we want to establish a compassion-based foundation for athletics, incorporating The Agony of Winning **Seven Strategies** will help build that foundation.

If everyone were committed to those Strategies, maybe the following event would not have happened. A high school coach in Dallas – the girls' head basketball coach at the Covenant School – could have used the tenets of **Strategy Four** to guide his coaching decisions. During the 2008-09 basketball season his team beat another school 100-0. He sent an e-mail to the "Dallas Morning News," saying he would not apologize "for a wide-margin winning when my girls played with honor and integrity." Perhaps they did, but it was his own ethical standards that I question. The administration fired Coach Micah Grimes, calling the blowout of Dallas Academy "shameful." A **Code of Ethics** is about having an overriding desire to do what is right. **Integrity** beckons us to practice restraint.

This coach hardly showed restraint and should probably revisit his understanding of the word **Integrity**. He actually showed a huge lack of respect for the game itself. Demonstrating respect for the higher truths of athletic competition is a great **leadership** model to exhibit. It would have been great to have his team just work on passing for one quarter, then maybe only a certain type of dribble. Lastly, might have instructed his players that only certain shots could be taken, maybe with the non-dominant hand. He could have called a time-out and showed incredible **leadership** by gathering the referees and opposing coach to communicate with empathy for them what his team was doing and why. Would it have been that difficult to employ this ethical, respectful tactic to the situation? In fact, this situation cried out for the application of **Strategy Four: The Agony of Winning Code of Ethics: Setting a Tone for Integrity, Respect, and Civility.**

The "who" and "why" of the athletic experience could have been highlighted while the players worked on specific "what" skills that needed to be improved upon. This is not rocket science.

While writing this book, I was reading a book by Michael Bernard Beckwith titled <u>Spiritual Liberation: Fulfilling your Soul's Potential</u>. In chapter 15, I came across a few concepts that I think are appropriate to the ethical concepts of **Integrity, Civility,** and **Respect.** The chapter is called "Mending Your Spiritual Manners on Planet Earth." Beckwith writes that *"manners are a system of respect ... in truth they are energy actions that carry a vibration which becomes a personal advertisement about who we are and what we value."* It means that it is important to be aware of "who" you are being, to be sure your actions are in alignment with who you say you are. In other words, your actions represent the truth of your "why," your motivations for playing.

He also quotes Emily Post – yes, sports fans, *that* Emily Post, the queen expert of etiquette. She says, "Manners are a sensitive awareness of the feeling of others." I call that empathy. People who practice the ethical standard of respect and civility have empathy. Beckwith goes on to quote Pier M. Forni, a professor at Johns Hopkins University and author of <u>Choosing Civility: The Twenty-Five Rules of Considerate Conduct:</u> *"I am absolutely convinced that everything including our thoughts, choices, behaviors and actions are energy and have a beneficial or harmful impact depending upon what the individual puts forth in every moment of every day."* Or in other words, the tone set by media, parents, coaches, and players in sports spreads feelings, whether positive or negative, throughout the sports world. All of us involved with athletics must be committed to a more positive, ethical, civil tone.

If you cannot respect yourself, you will be unable to demonstrate respect for others. The gateway to self-respect is having integrity. If you have incorporated the lessons learned with this principle, it has provided a great foundation. Once you have **Respect** for yourself, it is easy to demonstrate respect for others. The result is that "who" you are in your relationships with others will be someone who treats others in a manner that demonstrates respect even when there are disagreements.

Once you respect yourself it is easy to show consideration or appreciation for others. When your own actions and behavior demonstrate integrity and respect, it is easy to "treat people that way you'd like to be treated." This is the Golden Rule, after all. If everyone learned to apply and live by a code of ethics it would lead to more respectful, civil interactions among players, fans, teammates, parents, and coaches. As former Indiana Colts Coach Tony Dungy states, *"True respect starts with the way you treat others, and it is learned over a lifetime of acting with kindness, honor, and dignity."* It does not really matter how well you do the "what" of sports if you don't treat people well and have respect for them. This is a "who" you are being while you interact and compete with others, do you own a core value of respect for them and their point of view? Do you listen with empathy, do you respond with compassion? If so, then you are truly being respectful, not just acting respectfully.

Of course, in any human interaction the potential for disagreements is always present. However, this does not mean that in order to be "right" we react toward those with whom we disagree in an uncivil manner. To restore civility to our relationships we must learn to incorporate respect into our interactions. Sometimes people, including ourselves, are illogical, unreasonable, and ego-driven. I am not suggesting you allow others to step all over you. However, you can respectfully disagree and maintain integrity and civility.

Do we want unethical leadership? In a study titled, *"What Are Your Children Learning? The Impact of High School Sports on the Values and Ethics of High School Athletes,"* conducted by the Josephson Institute of Ethics in California, the report found some distributing data that support my contention. Here are a few of the findings:

- 65% of athletes (and 72% of football players) acknowledged cheating on exams.
- 43% of boys believe trash talking and showboating during games is acceptable behavior.
- 48% of baseball players believe it's acceptable for a coach to order a pitcher to throw at an opposing hitter.
- High school students involved in sports cheat in school at a higher rate than their classmates who aren't athletes.
- Nearly two-thirds (65%) of the boys and girls participating in sports cheated on an exam in the past year.

Whether this enhanced propensity to cheat is due to values that put winning over honesty, a reflection of pressures to stay eligible, or simply difficulties managing their time given the high demands of sports, the fact remains that for most kids, sports promotes rather than discourages cheating. The Josephson study also reveals the following information:

- Varsity athletes of both genders cheat at a higher rate than non-varsity athletes.
- Many coaches teach negative lessons. Despite the athletes' positive views of the character and intentions of their coaches, athletes revealed attitudes and conduct suggesting that many coaches are teaching negative lessons about cheating and bad sportsmanship. For example, 43% of the boys and 22% of girls think it is proper for a coach to teach basketball players how to illegally hold and push in ways that are difficult to detect (51% of boys in football, 49% in baseball and 47% in basketball agreed).
- Two-fifths (41%) of the boys and one-fourth of the girls (25%) saw nothing wrong with using a stolen playbook sent by an anonymous supporter before a big game. Baseball (49%) and football (48%) players were the most likely to approve of the use of the other team's playbook.
- More than one in three (37%) of the boys and one in five (20%) of girls think it is proper for a coach to instruct a player in football to fake an injury in order to get a needed time-out (44% of baseball and 43% of football players endorsed this strategy).
- More than two in five (41%) of boys and less than one quarter (23%) of girls think it is acceptable for a volleyball coach to say nothing when an official makes a mistake in the score that favors his team. Football and baseball players were considerably more likely to endorse this practice (50% and 49% respectively).

The Agony of Winning **Strategy Four Code of Ethics** is not a sometimes thing. It is not selective. It is the truth about the manner in which a person conducts his or her life. Michael Josephson makes this point nicely, *"I absolutely believe that the kinds of gamesmanship and unethical strategies that seem so trivial at the time produce young people who are not committed to honor and honesty. Our sports fields may be training the next generation of corporate villains. This is the kind of behavior that led to Enron, for example."* We do not want to be developing leaders who throw up their hands and succumb to the "end" justifies the "means" mentality. Are we training our future leaders, through their participation in athletics, that they must finish first no matter what it takes to get there? The world of athletics is presently training those types of leaders. As Josephson writes in his report, *"If you learn to play against the rules but in a way the officials don't notice, that isn't different than saying, 'Show you how to falsify your financial statements so nobody notices.'"*

I know that athletics can do better. Whether it is the media, parents, fans, coaches, or players, the lofty potential of sports to teach good, solid, ethical practices is not being fully utilized. This strategy should be taught to every parent and coach in America. Every player should be required to learn a **Code of Ethics**. This way when they become parents, high school, college or pro players, coaches, or sports writers, they understand the larger picture of this thing called athletic competition.

Ethics in athletics is not just theory. Ethics is a "who you are" step. It is an action step. It is a "how you are conducting yourself in any given moment" step. In order to be ethical there must be a set of moral standards, ethics that you apply to your decision making regardless of consideration about the outcome. You need to realize that ethical principles provide the foundation for values clarification, goal setting, and effective decision making. The nature of ethics is that they contain at their core the universal truth of integrity, civility, and respect. Not personal truth but "universal truth."

~~~~~~~~

Concept for Transforming the Agony of Winning to the Thrill of Winning:

Leadership starts with respect for oneself. Ethics in Leadership can and should be taught in the arena of athletics. It is important that players, coaches, and parents have a responsibility to teach ethical principles for Leadership.

~~~~~~~~

Question for Transforming the Agony of Winning to the Thrill of Winning:

What skills would you need to incorporate to ensure a response like that of Coach Pepicelli in a situation where you had to make a choice between winning and staying with your ethics and standards?

~~~~~~~~

Word for Transforming the Agony of Winning to the Thrill of Winning:

Willingness

9

The Sports Media

The Masters of Myth

I believe a lot of the negative change over the last 20 years originated in the media in all its various forms. In fact, this change in television, radio, and print rivals the uncivil behavior of parents. The core value of respect for others has been lost in the area of sports reporting. The media in large measure would do well to incorporate the principles found in **Strategy Four: The Agony of Winning Code of Ethics: Setting a Tone for Integrity, Respect, and Civility.** The sheer volume of broadcasting and the number of people who access it is unprecedented. The last two decades have seen the birth of all-sports talk radio; 24-hour cable TV sports coverage; and, let us not forget to mention bloggers, internet radio shows, and newspaper coverage of sports from every angle. Since there is a plethora of avenues for the sports fan to get information, the information they're getting is more provocative and lies on the edge of real journalism.

The danger is that journalism is so driven by the ratings for electronic media and by advertising dollars in the print media that the more outrageous the reporting the better. The end result in this "Shock Jock" style of sports news coverage is that accuracy and factual information are sometimes hedged in favor of a more glamorous story line. In the summer issue of the NCAA publication "Champions," Gary Brown writes, *"The potential for manipulation and exploiting subject matter is a lot greater when you're looking for ratings points."* He also cites a quote from Greg Bowers, a professor at the Missouri School of Journalism, in which he says, *"Merely reviewing what happened on the field of play wasn't as important since most of the audience already knew the outcome. The old reason for buying the newspaper is gone. What journalists are trying to do is create a new reason for buying the paper."* Bowers continued, *"That has meant giving readers something unique, and that change has resulted in a bent towards writers offering more inflammatory commentary and becoming more visibly a part of the story – perhaps even crossing the line from reporting to entertaining."* He continued, *"The traditional game story died years ago. Offering depth and analysis and telling the behind the scenes stories is where sports journalism has gone."*

As a result, in many ways the manner in which fans, parents, coaches, and players view sports has been molded by this type of sports news reporting. Many core values and the code of ethics present in eras gone by have been lost, along with the time-honored unwritten code of **Civility** and **Respect** in our interactions with each other.

One glance at the Philadelphia headlines gives all the evidence needed to drive this point home. Check out this tidy, little headline displaying the newspapers dissatisfaction toward Philadelphia Eagles quarterback Donovan McNabb, *"Stick a fork in him: McNabb is done."* This headline comes from the "Philadelphia Inquirer," referring to McNabb after a disappointing performance in one of the games. The reporter, Ashley Fox, wrote the article after the team had hit a bump in the road during the 2008 season. *"The likely scenario,"* she continues, *"is that Eagles will say thanks and goodbye to McNabb."* She is propagating a myth that is miles from the truth; the Eagles were not going to say goodbye to McNabb at season's end. I call this method of reporting, "The Art of Turning Assumptions into Truth."

In the article, Fox, the football expert, reveals that sad sack McNabb *"...hasn't overcome faulty coaching or bad play calling."* I guess she felt it was necessary to throw the head coach and the offensive coordinator under the bus with McNabb. You see, Fox is an equal opportunity critic. What really got on her nerves is that the uncaring rascal McNabb was not the least bit overcome with angst over the fact that the Eagles record over the last 4 games was a pathetic 2 wins, 1 loss, and 1 tie. That he was keeping his cool and offered the following perspective, that the offense's *"... confidence is high."* As a retort to McNabb's lack of anxiety, Fox noted in her commentary that, *"It will remembered that McNabb wasn't crying for a sense of urgency. Rather, he stayed true to form, even keel as if the ship wasn't sinking."* God knows that when the ship is sinking we all desire a captain who demonstrates urgency, fear, and anxiety so we will all follow with confidence. I know the last thing I want is some even-keel leader when things are not going well. Give me panic each and every time.

Donovan McNabb's calm comes from his perspective of the relative nature of sports. He knows deep down inside about his own worth as a person and a player. He also has a conviction that there are things that are greater, more important than being an NFL football player. He understands the principles that are taught in *Strategy Three: Maintaining a Balance of Intrinsic and Extrinsic Goals.* He puts his **Intrinsic** goals into action in his everyday life. There is a carry-over for him from the playing field to his life outside of the sport. He has deep spiritual and religious roots. He values being a good family man. It is important to him to be a good son, a good husband, and a good father. His relative calm about having a bad game or two, although very important to him, is not the "be all and the end all." That fact really irritates fans, sport writers, and the electronic media. He has had tremendous success playing football, but some of his proudest accomplishments can be found off the field. For example, through his efforts as a philanthropist, McNabb's dynamic personality, combined with an extraordinary work ethic, has produced DM5, the Donovan McNabb Foundation. McNabb's grandmother died of diabetes-related complications, and his father, Samuel, was diagnosed with type 2 diabetes years ago. In addition, a foundation headed by McNabb has donated $150,000 to the American Diabetes Association's youth camping program. This cause is dear to his heart.

What happens in the media is that a lot of assumptions are made and then presented to the general public for consumption. These assumptions are then written about and broadcast as if they were reality. Ashley Fox's article is a perfect example of this. She made an assumption that McNabb must not care if he is acting so cool while the team is struggling. The reader then perpetuates this assumption by believing he must not be very sensitive to the importance of winning, instead of the fact that he has it in perspective relative to the whole of his life. Then it becomes the truth that McNabb does not care enough to bring a Super Bowl win to Philly. I live and interact with people from the sports community in the Philly area, so I can tell you with certainty that this myth about McNabb is believed as the God's honest truth around these parts. His demeanor annoys Fox so she uses the largest newspaper in the Philly and South Jersey area as a platform to vent her anger.

The observer then looks for all the evidence they can find to support their assumptions. Let me share one with you. Often in tough situations, when he makes a mistake, McNabb will smile. A fan looking for an "I don't care attitude" from him will use this as supporting evidence to that truth. I have heard this repeated over and over again. That notion is absurd. McNabb is not smiling because he does not care. It is just his way. It is most likely a stress-relief mechanism for him. I also believe that in the larger scheme of his life he has put a fumble or a pass interception in proper perspective. However, I want to be careful here and not make any "assumptions." I do know that fans could use a heavy dose of the message inside **Strategy Four: The Agony of Winning Code of Ethics: Setting a Tone for Integrity, Respect, and Civility.**

After the NFC playoff loss to Arizona, Phil Sheridan writes in the "Philadelphia Inquirer," "*Champions write their own legacy. Everyone else's gets written for them. That is the reality* (there you have it that is reality, Phil said so*). For Andy*

Reid and Donovan McNabb, the coach and quarterback, who reached five NFC championship games together and will now be remembered mostly for losing them and a Super Bowl." There is another reality not covered in the story, the absolutely amazing accomplishments that this coach and this quarterback have achieved.

Sheridan is assuming that the losses should be the most memorable aspects of the careers of these two men. The readers accept his assumption, because the expert said so, and they take it personally. They are diehard fans, so they believe this should be the truth about the two mens' careers and gossip it loud and clear, as many times as possible. Even other players and coaches begin to believe the assumptions. All of this is a perfect recipe for the "nothing is good enough, what have you done for me lately" attitude that permeates sports today. The drive for being No. 1 is given all the credence it needs from these types of messages. There is no place but 1st place. The listening public includes young athletes and coaches and parents. It is a dangerous perspective from which to view the purity of athletic competition. The spirit of sport is lost in all the negative verbiage, spoken, and written. What also gets lost is the message found in **Strategy Two: Competing with Purpose and Passion** for the young athlete. The purpose is not just to be No. 1. This kind of reporting reduces the athletic experience to that singular measurement.

"Inquirer columnist" John Gonzales wanted to make sure that the Philly faithful knew that other cities suffer from a lack of achievement so he introduced the Buffalo Bills' futility to the adoring public. The headline provided by the newspaper for his article is priceless: *"Glory Instead of Misery, Adulation Instead of Scorn, Winning Instead of yet another NFC Title*

The Agony of Winning   •

Game Defeat?" He writes, *"Marv Levy, Jim Kelly (coach and quarterback) and the rest of the Buffalo Bills from the early 90's will high five each other and raise a glass in the Eagles' honor. Sure the Bills lost four Super Bowls and became a national punch line. But as the Eagles have so kindly demonstrated by going 1-4 in NFC championship games, there are worse things."* Gonzales is putting his belief out into the public that these two franchises are losers, in spite of unprecedented success, the assumption being that the only real winners are those who are successful in the Super Bowl. That assumption becomes truth for the general public when this kind of disregard for the reality of success enjoyed by these two franchises is imparted daily for consumption by readers eager for bad news.

Because of cable TV, there is total access to the ins and outs of sports. Unfortunately, there is a lack of a value called **Integrity** to go along with this nonstop reporting. Total access has not brought with it the personal responsibility for what is being spoken and written. Today we are provided with 24-hour commentary on the world of sports. Everyone has become an expert as a result of this ongoing dissection of every game, every player, and each play in the game. I mean every play. In an effort to fill the hours upon hours of pre-game, during the game, and post-game time slots, the commentators give the viewer a bird's-eye view. A thought verbalized over and over again by the commentator becomes truth, and the viewer believes it.

The basic effect is that an entire generations of fans, players, and parents have become self-appointed experts on the ins and outs of athletics. They have a front row seat into the smallest details for the upcoming game as well as the players and coaches who are participating. They are experts by association; they are included in the action. They are taking the assumptions, delivered by the media, with a lack of respect and a negative tone, and making them the truth. The viewers are becoming experts in their own right. After all, they have honed their skills through the grueling curriculum provided by ESPN and other nonstop sports networks.

I was watching former NFL great Michael Strahan and current Fox sports authority on a pre-game show before the Eagles NFC Championship. Eagles coach Andy Reid was being interviewed by another reporter about the upcoming game. After the interview, the viewer was taken back to the studio so Strahan and the rest of the studio crew could give us a little more insight into Reid This is mainly because the fans need an expert to interpret the interview for us. Instead, Strahan treated the public to a disrespectful statement about the head coach, as well as a total lack of civility in his delivery. He said about Reid, who was wearing shorts for the interview: *"There are only two things that should be on Andy's legs, pants or barbecue sauce."* That is very funny, Michael. I was disgusted by the comment. In the more civil era in which he played, he was not subject to those kinds of degrading remarks. Why, I ask, is that comment necessary on national television? ***Strategy Four: the Agony of Winning Code of Ethics: Setting a Tone for Integrity, Respect, and Civility*** would have come in handy for Strahan.

I know that we cannot turn back the hands of time to a simpler era. But I would be remiss if I did not reach back a little and point out that a decorum existed at one time in the media that provided a system of checks and balances. So the following commentary takes us back to a different era to illustrate the point that the Agony of Winning **Strategy Four** was alive and well in a different time and place.

In January 1968, an "Esquire" magazine article written by Leonard Schecter titled "The Toughest Man" depicted legendary Green Bay Packers coach Vince Lombardi in a very negative manner given the era in which it was written. In his book, When Pride Still Mattered, author David Maraniss, includes some paraphrases from the article written by Schecter: "... Lombardi was described as swearing at his players, casually dismissing their pain and injury, arguing with Marie (his wife) and generally acting bellicose if not abusive." I think the next sentence that Maraniss writes speaks volumes, "when considered from the remove of decades, Schecter's piece seems relatively tame." He is right. These types of comments written today would not draw much attention.

The response to the article by another reporter of that era speaks to why we need The Agony of Winning **Strategies** and to reach back to days gone by to rediscover some compassion-based athletics. Another sports journalist of the era found the Schecter article disrespectful and uncivil. The person was Dick Schaap. Maraniss reports that Schaap read the piece while he was editing the manuscript of Jerry Kramer's book Instant Replay. Schaap thought Schecter was mostly off in the tone he had assigned to the article. He deemed the article too negative, and said it lacked **Civility**. Once again, the Schecter article was tame by the modern era of reporting. Maraniss continued, "There was almost nothing in the magazine article that did not echo something in Jerry Kramer's diary, but Kramer's assessment of Lombardi was more complex and forgiving." Maraniss quotes Schaap as saying, "There were a lot of truths in it, but it was too far one way. It may have been accurate, but it wasn't fair." Schecter made some assumptions about Lombardi that were based on his own personal prejudice and presented them to the public. This was very juicy stuff back in 1968; however, Schaap had manners, if you will. He wasn't disputing the facts of the article, just the negative energy and lack of **Civility** demonstrated by Schecter. Schaap was also demonstrating respect for Coach Lombardi. He was having empathy and compassion because he knew Lombardi and he knew that the coach saw himself not just as a brutal football coach. *"He preferred to be known as a teacher, leader, bearer of the Insignias Medal, the man who had preached nobility of sport,"* **according to XX (Kevin - who said this???).**

A reporter trained in the aspects of the **Strategy Four:** *the* **Agony of Winning Code of Ethics: Setting a Tone for Integrity, Respect, and Civility** might decide to take the comment made by Michael Strahan about Andy Reid's legs and report the same facts about Andy Reid's weight with a different tone, a more empathic and civil tone. Maybe the reporter would comment on the fact that Reid is a good man, a man who is passionate about his profession. If Strahan wanted to set a civil tone he might have married that comment with a statement about the fact that there is something INTRINSICALLY wrong with a grown man coaching a sport and sleeping in his office due to the amount of hours he works. Ethical reporting may have required Strahan to comment on how sad it is that Reid has gained so much weight, as he tries to cope with the stress of coaching in a town of sports-crazed fans in Philadelphia.

In 1968, when there was a still some civil decorum in sports reporting, Schecter wrote about Lombardi, who was a big man, as one who had *"a bit of a weight problem and walks with his belly sucked in and his chest expanded like a pigeon's."* No mention of barbecuing any body parts like Strahan suggests we do with Reid's legs. However, that tone seemed out of line with the reporting **Ethics** of the day so Schaap rebutted and challenged Schecter's choice of tone while presenting his point of view. That is a direct contrast to the rest of the crew on the set when Strahan made his remarks. The other analysts in the studio laughed or shook their heads while laughing. None of them challenged him like Schaap had challenged Schecter. They were probably afraid they might lose their lucrative contracts if they did. Well, there is a price tag that comes with a **Code of Ethics**. Sometimes it requires that we step out of the box and make a tough choice between what we want, i.e., shock effect, a big contract, winning and losing, and **"who"** we want to be. An individual with high ethical standards does not waiver for the convenience of avoiding tough situations.

Sometimes these viewpoints are justified with such statements as "well, this is big time athletics and it is a business" and only No. 1 counts. Sorry, but that does not wash; the business of athletics still has a responsibility to the positive values that sports should be teaching. The ego works hard to justify these situations. Statements like, "Well, it goes with the territory, they know before they get involved, or this is the way it is." Baloney. The negative tone set and perpetuated by the media is unacceptable and needs to be changed. It means establishing a **Code of Ethics** under which the "business" of sports can operate. That code is presented in *Strategy Four: the Agony of Winning Code of Ethics: Setting a Tone for Integrity, Respect, and Civility.* Who will be the first in the media to restore some class to the coverage of athletics?

It is important to note here that living an ethically guided life does not mean we never fail or make mistakes. Operating under the umbrella of universal truths does not mean we will not make errors of judgment. It does mean that when mistakes are made, we can change course. We can make amends and apologize if it is necessary to get back on the track of integrity, respect, and civility.

I remember a news article written about my high school basketball team in 1970. Our head coach, Pat Luciano, whom all the players loved and respected, said some things to a reporter after a very frustrating loss. Coach Luciano was an intense person and very demanding. I loved playing for him and would run through a wall for him if he told me that it would help the team. Some reporters were not fond of him because they deemed his methods too harsh. They made an assumption, like Schecter did about Lombardi, that his methods of coaching were over the top. They were unaware of his own application of **Strategy Two: Competing with Purpose and Passion** and **Strategy Three: Maintaining a Balance of Intrinsic and Extrinsic Goals.** However, his players were very aware that there was something about Coach Luciano that ran much deeper that his win-loss record. There was not one player I knew of who felt that Coach was over the top; just intense and passionate. After we lost to Warren Hills in the state tournament the headline the next day read, *"Luciano charges Dover with Choke."* My heart sank when I read that. The article quoted Coach Luciano as saying, *"We just can't play under pressure."* Luciano went on. *"Have you ever seen anything like this in your life? This is the worst game we have played all year."* This kind of reporting was unusual in 1970, especially when reporting on a high school game. However, it is very mild by today's standards.

I have always thought the reporter wanted to embarrass

Coach, even though this same reporter had written some favorable articles about my friend Danny Benz and me just two weeks earlier. Coach was frustrated and the reporter knew it. The reporter wrote in the article, *"So what had started out as the most productive season in Dover basketball history ends on a dismal note. The Tigers were 10-1 before hitting the skids harder than a banker in the Depression, losing seven of their last twelve."*

Once again having **Integrity** and living with a **Code of Ethics** does not mean you do not make mistakes. Coach realized his mistake by commenting so soon after the frustrating loss. He did what a man with a **Code of Ethics** does; he took the steps necessary to demonstrate his commitment to walk his talk. He showed the team **Respect** and demonstrated a sense of **Civility** by writing to the paper's sports editor to set the record straight. The reporter countered with his own lack of civility toward Luciano by providing this comment preceding the coach's published letter to the editor, *"The prowess of Luciano as a high school basketball coach goes without question. What is in question, however, is the tact employed by a high school coach no matter what good fortune or adversity may occur."* This reporter could not wait to print what Coach had said in total frustration after the game. I am also sure that he was not happy that his editor had decided to print Coach's apology to a team that loved him.

Here is a partial text of Coach Luciano's letter to the editor:

> *"The boys who were the mainstay of the team all year I have literally lived with at times and have come to know each boy as I have my own. I will always have a deep*

regard for them because of their personal character, for their dedication to the game of basketball, for the example they set for younger players coming along and lastly because of the ability to come back fighting despite losses and personal disappointments. They may have lost a few key games along the way, but they are and always will be, true gentlemen despite an excitable and demanding coach."

I would not have wanted Coach to be any other way. As I said, we all loved him. If the reporter had asked any of us we would have told him that we let Coach down.

I am not sure any media outlet today would have the **Integrity** of John Lykem, the sports editor of the "Daily Advance," to print a letter like that. The media needs to go back and rediscover that spirit of civility and fairness. This particular article, left alone without rebuttal, makes an assumption about the players and the coach, decides it's the truth, writes about it, the reader reads it, gossips about it, and makes it the truth. I am thankful for the era I played in, where the sports editor believed in the tenets found in **Strategy Four:** *the Agony of Winning Code of Ethics: Setting a Tone for Integrity, Respect, and Civility* and printed the real truth about the players on the Dover Tigers basketball team. He also gave Coach Luciano a chance to model grace and vulnerability.

Once again, we can go back and rediscover the feeling state of civility, respect, and integrity that existed in another time, not that long ago. I often tell parents, coaches, and players that what is missing in athletics today is depth in our relationships with each other. This is certainly true of the relationship between the media and coaches. There is a lot of tension between the two.

There was a time when the media and coaches got to know each other a little and actually formed a relationship based on **Integrity and Respect** and had a **Civil** tone. In speaking about his early journalistic career, Malcolm Moran, a Penn State journalism professor and former "New York Times" reporter, says he is concerned that the relationship between writers and their subjects has suffered so. He describes how he got to know present Duke University basketball coach Mike Krzyzewski when he was at West Point. He said there were not more than a dozen people covering Coach K after the games. He also stated that there was more willingness from the coaches to spend quality time with the reporters. *"You'd have Mike, Lou Carresecca, Jim Valvano, and would linger a little while, so in addition to the structured remarks, you had a chance to introduce yourself, get to know them, do a story on them, they see your work,"* Moran said. *"And that led to understanding, and that led to a chance to repair damage if there was a controversial topic or if you made a mistake – at least there was a little foundation there that allowed you to talk it over."* A common **Civility** can be re-established, but it takes a measure of willingness on each side.

Sometimes the disdain for each other demonstrated by coaches and reporters is startling. Young athletes, parents/fans, and youth coaches are witnessing this lack of respect and registering it as the norm.

Concept for Transforming the Agony of Winning to the Thrill of Winning:

In sports today there is a general lack of concern for others. It is time to adopt an attitude that reflects respect for others. A civil decorum will not diminish in any way the competitive nature of athletics. It will enhance the experience for all.

Question for Transforming the Agony of Winning to the Thrill of Winning:

Why is it important to for the media to re-establish decorum, civility, and respect in their reporting? How would that be beneficial to parents, coaches, and athletes?

Word for Transforming the Agony of Winning to the Thrill of Winning:

Respect

10

The Season Without End

Oh those lazy, hazy days of summer. I remember them well. Now those were the days. No school, no science or math, no bells ringing to signal it was time to move to another class. The summer months were a respite from adults managing every minute of the day. As an aspiring athlete, to me the summer months were also a time to take a break from the coach's instruction — to experiment with new shots, play games without a scoreboard, fans, standings, and, most of all, adult regulation.

Almost without fail I played basketball every night all summer. I did not need a schedule to tell me when to play. My brothers and other teammates played on the playground, pickup ball at Crescent Field on Second Street in Dover, N.J., with a wide range of interesting characters. There were guys like "Jumping Jack," the Wright brothers, Robert and Roger, Jimmy Simms, most of them unemployed; some were out on bail and others were drug addicts. Some had a few teeth here and there or smelled like cheap booze sometimes, but they all loved basketball and the playground.

Then there were older guys from high school and college who loved to play ball and provided us younger guys with tremendous competition. Playing against all of these guys helped us improve our game. In addition, there were even younger guys, like my brother Brian, who were looking to challenge the status quo and put out the warning that their time was coming. However, we set the schedule for when we were going to play and there were no adults in charge of anything, not how we set up the rules of the game, not how we picked teams, not what part of our game we were going to work on, and not how long we were going to play. This is the exact opposite of what I see today with the organized summer schedule games. When I was growing up, the parents did not set up on the sidelines in their lawn chairs and have a tailgate party to watch us play our pickup games. We were left alone by adults so we could be kids.

Make no mistake about it, we were very competitive, but we were taking a break from the pressures of games played in uniforms, in front of an audience, with a scoreboard, screaming cheerleaders, parents, and coaches, with their egos and careers hanging onto every play like their lives depended on it. In summer we took a break from all that. It was in a literal sense a vacation.

Oh, do not get me wrong, I loved playing for "real" with all the trappings. I thrived in those situations, from October to March. In today's world of athletics, summer means something else. Off season means training for the one sport the athlete has chosen to be THE sport for them to pursue to get that college scholarship. Thus we have THE SEASON WITHOUT END.

As I have written over and over in this book, in the last 20 years or so the athletic community has placed so much emphasis on a singular measurement of success, becoming No. 1, that we have developed a breeding ground for the participants to have created an uncommon expectation of success in athletic competition. What is occurring is an over-the-top reaction to losing, bad performances, coaching decisions, referees, etc. Conversely, I find there to be a much muted positive response to playing well, winning, good performance, etc. This is because the athletic community has allowed the total attachment to the **Extrinsic** goals of athletic competition. The **Intrinsic** value of loving to compete for the pure, unadulterated experience of playing has been replaced with a huge pressure to perform. There has been at least a limited incorporation of the Agony of Winning **Strategy Three: Maintaining a Balance of Intrinsic and Extrinsic Goals,**

We have an arms race going on in the world of sports because of an overriding fear adults have that another individual or team is doing something in the off season that they are not. That something just may give that someone else an advantage. Parents, coaches, and ultimately players are in an amazing race to ensure the outcome they desire, before someone else beats them to it. So parents and coaches subject their children and players to an overindulgence of training opportunities. The paradox is that desire or the spirit of participation is often dead on arrival, when and if, the desired outcome is reached. By the time they are 16 or 17, they have played 6,000 organized games and competition has lost its ability to excite the athlete. My private coaching practice has been full of scholarship and non-scholarship players just tired of playing. I wonder why? It is because the season never really ends. The Agony of Winning system uses **Strategy Five: Overcoming the Pressure to Succeed** *to guide coaches, players, and parents to a more peaceful approach to athletic competition.*

In 2008 I worked with a basketball team of 16- and 17-year-old girls who had zero desire to play anymore. The whole team lack passion for playing. They had played and trained with each other basically every summer on organized travel teams since they were in fourth grade. They were very good players, and expectations for the team were very high. The players couldn't care less about the upcoming season, and the coaches were dumbfounded that the players were not excited. I was hired to conduct my Agony of Winning workshop and we spent a tremendous amount of time on **Strategy Five: Overcoming the Pressure to Succeed.** Through the success formula of the Agony of Winning system, the coaches and players were able to rediscover their own lost spirit of sports. In addition, they left with a valuable, powerful renewal of their care, concern, appreciation, and love for each other. They then exceeded the early season expectations placed upon them. But what is more important is they had fun doing it.

In the workshops, the players and coaches revealed a collective sentiment that they almost always have underlying anxiety about performing up to expectations. They were not talking about excitement; they had been feeling anxious. There is a huge difference between excitement, which is positive, and anxiety, which is negative. One brings a sense of joy, the other relief or major disappointment once the competition is over. The spirit and integrity of sports is threatened by this **Pressure to Succeed**. The response by coaches and parents had been to do more; more clinics, more individual instruction, and more camps to develop skills. The idea being that more training will help the players get better. The reality is that we are creating a generation of zombies in athletic uniforms. What is not being recognized is that along with the time commitment to get better come higher and higher expectations for performance.

The Pressure to Succeed and the amount of the time athletes are under that pressure is greater now than at any time in athletic history. We need a fresh pair of lenses to give us a new perspective of sports that makes having fun while competing a priority. In the hours the team and I worked together on **Strategy Five: *Overcoming the Pressure to Succeed,*** I was able to explain to the team that positive emotions such as appreciation, care, compassion, care, joy, and peace create a more relaxed approach to competition. We worked with the team to place more emphasis on the joy, fun, and other **Intrinsic** benefits of competition found in ***Strategy Three: Maintaining a Balance of Intrinsic and Extrinsic Goals.*** The athletes were able to see that this perspective would produce positive feelings they could use to reduce the **Pressure to Succeed**.

The Agony of Winning **Strategy Five** urged them to change their perspective and incorporate a new attitude in regard to the amount of time required to be an athlete. This new perspective would help them change the way they looked at the opponents, teammates, themselves, and conditioning. Hating their competitors, being jealous of a teammate, degrading their own abilities, or hating a drill or exercise will all quickly turn to a negative experience while competing. These were all **distractions** that lead to the **pressure to succeed**. We also worked with them on taking a different approach to the never-ending season, to take more breaks and schedule down time. But more important was to not look just at the **extrinsic** value of the training, but at what the training was providing for internal personal growth. We asked them to use positive feeling tools like learning to appreciate themselves, teammates, coaches, and competitors. These perspectives helped the athletes deal with the grind of the never-ending season as well as the **pressure to succeed**.

Imagine the implications on your performance when you repeatedly feel hatred for a competitor, running hills, wind sprints, exercise, weights, practice, and playing. I explained to the team that these negative frames of references were actually providing **Distractions** and making the time commitment even more arduous. I took them through exercise after exercise to show them how to eliminate **Distractions**. Simply changing the feelings from negative ones like frustration to positive ones like appreciation and gratitude helped provide them with more physical strength and energy, resulting in a more powerful, flowing performance.

The following quote from their coach sums up the results of our workshop on the season. The quote also illustrates the fact that it is never too late to restore the spirit of playing and the Thrill of Winning at the same time.

> *"One of the biggest things you do is to help the girls better understand and deal with the outside distractions and*

pressures, especially their time commitment and their parents' expectations. The outlet this program provided for them an opportunity for them to share, explore, and talk about the pressures they feel to perform well. I can assure you that the burdens and pressures they feel are amazing.

The biggest thing that happened last year for the girls was that the experience really became more about them and less about other people and outside pressure, distractions, and expectations. It became more about a fun high school experience vs. the result. The amazing thing is that the results became more meaningful as we enjoyed the experience more! By focusing on the experience of being together at practice, team dinners, meetings, bus rides, etc. vs. only the winning and losing, we played better and enjoyed it more. Even in our losses, we were resilient and we dwelled less on the result and more on the next challenge. It was fun again!"

I am acutely aware that most adults, parents, coaches, and fans have no idea about the time commitment required of athletes today. They have more demands on their structured time than any previous generation. This is especially true in the last 20 years. They do not play more hours than we did as young athletes, but all of their play is structured with non-stop coaching and adult supervision.

The following is an e-mail from a kind mother to the head coach at the high school her daughter, then in fourth grade, would eventually attend. Notice that in the second sentence the mom mentions a softball tournament. The woman is writing this e-mail to the basketball coach regarding his summer program. Also, the MBA mentioned is a structured basket-ball league. Notice that the mom also mentions gymnastics. OK, we have softball, basketball, and gymnastics, but not in rotating seasons with a beginning and an end for each. This is a never-ending season of three sports being played at once. Remember, this student/athlete is in fourth grade.

Coach:

I looked over the schedule and there is only one conflict that I can see — the weekend of June 19 & 20. She is scheduled to play in a softball tournament that weekend, but I am sure we can try to work around the game schedules. I won't know until it's closer to that date, but we will do everything we can to be there. Her softball team has moved up to another age bracket so it is going to be a rebuilding year – we will see how that progresses. Practice nights are perfect!!! No MBA or gymnastics on those days — at least through the end of April. Elyse's MBA state tournament is the 1st weekend in May so I don't know what her practice schedule will be after that but they usually try to keep it the same through the end of the school year.

Please read the rest of the e-mail carefully. This is a coach who has adopted the Agony of Winning System for his high school team and will be introducing it in the summer program for grades four through eight. The never-ending season is here to stay, that is not going to change. However, **Strategy Five: Overcoming the Pressure to Succeed** will help restore and replenish the energy of the athletes and coaches by elimi-nating the **Distractions** and stressful feelings that accompany such a demanding schedule. This parent is in touch with the positive feelings the coach carries with him as he deals with his own version of the never-ending season. He holds positive this perspective because he cares about the "who" of his players. He has adopted the principles of the Agony of Winning **Strategy Two: Competing with Purpose and Passion.** He makes sure their passion is considered by reminding them of the "why" of competition for himself, as well as his players. He sets **Intrinsic** goals with them, so the time commitment is given a richer meaning. Their training is not just a never-ending regimen of teaching the technical skills we refer to as the "what." Important concepts he coaches with are found in *Strategy One: Agony of Winning Triangle: The Who, What, and Why of Athletics.* All of these principles are reflected in his interactions with the people his program involves. Here is more from the parent of this fourth-grade athlete.

> *"I enjoyed talking with you last night. I always walk away with a positive insight after talking with you and after the disappointing weekend we had with the MBA team, I think it was just what Elyse and I needed."*

The coach will employ the Agony of Winning **Strategy Five: Overcoming the Pressure to Succeed** for this 9-year-old athlete. He will assure the player that a disappointing weekend can be expected when competing and it should not become a **distraction** or negative feeling for her. The time to move on started with the end of the last game of the disappointing weekend. The e-mail ends with these thoughts from the parent:

> *"I would never talk discouragingly about MBA or their program, but I do see a difference with Elyse and her*

passion for playing the game. I want her to continue to develop her skills and work on her game, but I also want her to continue to have fun and enjoy the game she is so passionate about. We all are looking forward to her playing with you and the girls again this year. Thanks for the opportunity & please let us know if you need anything or if we can help in any way!!!"

Have a great day,

Lori

Lori makes a statement in the e-mail that illustrates the essentional nature of the Agony of Winning system. She writes, ***"I want her to continue to develop her skills and work on her game, but I also want her to continue to have fun and enjoy the game she is so passionate about."*** What Lori has done is set some **Intrinsic** goals for herself, as a parent, in regard to Elyse's playing career. She has the spirit-renewing goal of wanting her daughter to be passionate, and have fun while she works on her skills. She knows this coach features those **Intrinsic** goals inside the delivery of his highly successful, competitive program. I am going to add to her statement and say that her goals should be reflective in the goals of every parent who has an athletic child competing in any organized sport. This simple e-mail illustrated that the Agony of Winning workshop should be a requirement for all parents before their child is allowed to compete.

I was conducting a leadership workshop for a football team and coaches at a high school in South Jersey in 2007. The team and head coach were there and we were talking about commitment. The head coach reacted when I complimented the players on being members of a generation of the most committed athletes in the history of competitive sports. I told them that in relation to working on the "what," the amount of time they put into training is unprecedented. I also told them they are lacking in other aspects of their competitive experience compared to athletes of eras gone by – the aspects of the "why" and "who" side of participation. However, despite that the yearlong training regimen expected of them is different than any other time in sports history. At that, the coach hit the roof and said he felt like the players needed to be more committed, more dedicated to his training regimen. He said, *"Sometimes it is like pulling teeth to get them to the summer workouts."*

Those workouts are all summer long, but they do not start in the summer after a break from training. Those workouts are really just a continuation of the winter and spring workouts the team is required to attend after the fall football season ends. In addition, after school gets out, they must play in the 7 on 7 touch football league twice a week. The 7 on 7 league is against other schools and all coaches are present. Let us not forget that the parents are lining up on the sidelines sharpening their skills for the upcoming season as well. We cannot expect the parents to jump into judgment and criticism without some preseason work. The July 7 on 7 league is a good time for the parents to analyze whether the right plays are being run for Junior. You know Coach, the kinds of plays that are going to be needed next fall if Junior is going to reach his full college scholarship potential.

I responded by asking Coach the following question, *"Well, let's take a look at this, what years did you play high school football?"* He said he had played in the late 1970's. I continued my questioning, *"In the spring of 1978 what were* you doing?" He answered, *"Hanging out with my friends, going to the baseball games and track meets."* I responded, *"Fun, wasn't it?"* A smile came to his face as he remembered how much fun it was to experience those moments as a teenager. I had another question, *"What were you doing in late June, July and August in the late 1970s?"* Coach continued to smile as he said, *"I was going down to the beach with my friends, swimming in the ocean, throwing the football around. We played pickup games of touch football and I worked my summer job."* OK, I went for the close on this conversation. *"So Coach,"* I asked, *"who is more committed, as you put it, your era of athlete or the modern day athlete? Who was putting in more time and being asked to sacrifice more?"*

The players in the room liked the idea that Coach had no alternative but to answer that his players in 2007 had far less free time and more demands on them than the athletes of his era. The Coach spent the spring and summer months refreshing his mind, body, and spirit. Conversely, the players he coached are working out and being asked to draw endlessly from the well of their mind, body, and spirit without replenishing the source. It amazes me that parents and coaches do not recognize that the fun and excitement of starting a new season is nonexistent because the athletes are engaged in a SEASON WITHOUT END. Instead of moving from one sport to another, the athletes are moving from one kind of training for one sport to another. This is hardly the same thing. We did a heavy dose of lessons from **Strategy Five: Overcoming the Pressure to Succeed** with this group of players. They were well aware of what was expected of them as they commited their time to training. And the overriding message they had been receiving was that the training had better lead to more wins.

The overregulation of preseason and post season training is out of control on almost all levels of competition right down to the youngest athletes. This attitude of more is better once again filters its way down from the higher levels of competition. I never recruited a player in the summer months when I was coaching college basketball. That was just 20 years ago. I used the summer to recharge my own batteries. And resting always worked. I was always excited when the new school year started and the players came back to campus from a summer spent with their families and friends from their home town. In college athletics today, summer is as busy as the academic year. The coaches are in their off season job of evaluating future prospects on the playing fields and courts all over the world. The players are led to believe that if they want to secure that elusive college scholarship, they better dedicate their summer to being seen by the college coaches. This is not going to change and it is why I spend time in the workshops on the principles in **Strategy Two: Competing with Purpose and Passion,** to enable the athletes to keep their energy when they need it most.

As one local New Jersey high school basketball player, Mike Bersch, put it when discussing why he keeps such an intense summer schedule, *"This is when you really get seen,"* he said, referring to his AAU team. *"In high school, there may be one or two Division 1 players. But with AAU (college coaches) can come out and see a lot at one time. You need to play AAU to be seen."* So there goes the summer for parents, players, and coaches. Bersch, in addition to practicing and playing in the summer with his high school team, Rancocas Valley, does the same for his AAU team, the New Jersey Cyclones. The team is headquartered about 20 miles away from his home. *"It's hard,"* he said. *"I'll practice during the day with my AAU team, and that takes up most of my time. I usually get a ride up to Monmouth (20 miles from home) and then we practice for probably three hours. And then I get home, I'll go over to L.A. Fitness and lift for a while."* The conflict of his AAU and his high school summer schedule was evident in his next statement: *"I've missed a couple games* (with his high school team), *but I usually have practices on Tuesdays and games on Monday and Wednesday."* Mike did not get to play much his senior year. His season was lost through a series of injuries, one of which was a separated shoulder. I am not sure if the three-hour AAU practice compromised his weightlifting experience after practice at L.A. Fitness or not. Maybe it was his high school practice schedule being squeezed into the time between L.A. Fitness and AAU. Or maybe he slept on it wrong while he was being driven the 40-mile round trip to Monmouth, N.J., for those practices. It would be hard to prove that over training had anything to do with Bersch's injury-riddled senior year. He did, however, get his college scholarship even if his high school team did not do as well without him.

Overtraining, however, is dimming the fun of playing. Yes, remember playing for fun? Another prominent high school basketball player, Ashley Durham, another star player from New Jersey says, *"The hardest part is having fun."* Her long hours and training sessions are a part of her normal life, she says, just like brushing her teeth and resting her head on a pillow. I would concur that it would be hard to find fun in the work-like setting that sports has become. Oh, and by the way there is nothing normal about this. There is something gone wild about sports when, as Ashley puts it, *"The hardest part is having fun."* That is insane.

Injuries are another side issue in the training regimen of today's so called under-committed athletes experiencing the never-ending season. Here is an observation from Coach Anson Dorrance, head womens' soccer coach at North Carolina, in a *New York Times* article on this topic. *"Everybody's got a tournament. There's the Raleigh Shootout, the Surf Cup in Southern California, and ding, ding, ding, they're everywhere. So now girls are going somewhere every two or three months and playing these inordinate numbers of matches. And you know what? They're just playing to survive. And survival is not just the five games in three days. It's the two and three weeks following. They've got a niggling this and a niggling that – sprained ankle, aching backs. They are overplayed and they are never rested."*

Because athletes are picking one sport to specialize in as early as age 8, the training is more intense and the strain placed on the anatomy is dangerous. It is really out of control. If more high-profile coaches would get on board and speak out against these methods, it could help. Parents obsessed with their children's athletic performance could ease up a little. An article written by Lauren Neergaard, points out in an article written for the NCAA magazine, *Champion*, that, *"3.5 million children 14 and under receive treatment for sports-related injuries each year. Along with sprains and strains are a lot of overuse injuries – stress fractures, tendonitis, and cartilage damage."* Twenty years ago these were adult injuries, mostly affecting college and pro players.

Today it has fast-forwarded past the high school athlete right down to Little League and Pee Wee football. We live in an era where we see 13-year-old gymnasts who sometimes miss school so they can train nonstop, with lower back stress fractures. We have teenage runners who end up with stress fractures because of the year-long pounding their legs endured before puberty. In Neergaard's article, she points out the fact that the torn anterior cruciate ligament *"...was long thought a rarity in childhood. But among males, one in five; the figure is 30 percent among females."*

Once again quoting Fred Barnett, *"What are we doing to our children in the name of sports?"*

There was a time when the never-ending season meant something else. There was a rotation of sports played and organized by kids for their own pleasure or two or three sports stars moving with vigor from sport to sport. At an Agony of Winning forum, an audience member, Ed Maroon, who was the commissioner of the youth basketball program that I featured in another chapter of this book, stood up to ask a question. Ed is a really good man and truly wants to do the right thing for his child in relation to athletics. He was distraught as he spoke during the question and answer portion of the program. First he said he had been told by many people in the community that if he did not enroll his daughter in the travel program, she would never be a member of the high school program. He said he did not want to enroll his 9-year-old in that program because she would have to give up other activities to play year-round. He asked for advice. The panel suggested he not tap into that fear, that if his daughter was good enough she would not be left off the team in high school. I asked him if he was willing to put the rest of his daughter's life on hold for the next four years while they traveled every weekend to play tournaments.

I also said, *"The activities are not the only thing you will give up. Our children are giving up their childhoods. They are giving up the chance to just play for playing's sake. They are over-trained and over-committed. The burn out rate for young athletes is at an all-time high. It is not that athletes play more than we did 20 years ago. It is that they are playing more under pressure, evaluation, and coaching than any era in sports. We played every day, all day. It was very competitive. However, there were no adults around, we were not being coached ad nauseam every second by an adult. These kids' parents had other things to do than live out their own dreams on the backs of young kids."*

Ultimately, Ed decided his daughter needed to play travel league basketball in order to have a future in basketball. I cannot say I blame him. Not only is his daughter playing, he is the coach of the travel team here in Medford, New Jersey He felt the pressure because it appears mandatory for children to devote their lives to one sport by age 10. **Strategy Five: Overcoming the Pressure to Succeed** is an Agony Strategy that Ed would benefit from as his daughter embarks on her travel team career. Sadly, this mentality is here to stay. With this fact in mind, it is imperative that the Agony of Winning system be in place in all youth sports.

We are losing something when our athletes are being asked to give up other aspects of their lives to compete nonstop. In an article in *USA Today*, guest columnist Patrick Welsh, a teacher at T.C. Williams High School in Alexandria, Va., writes, *"If, in the 1950's the push for kids to specialize had been anything like it is today, we may have never heard of Jim Brown, who is universally considered the greatest running back in NFL history."* Brown was a multi-sports star at Manhasset High School in Long Island, NY. He continues, *"Brown averaged 38 points a game in basketball, but he also played baseball, lacrosse and football. Any kid today good enough to put up 38 a game would face insurmountable pressures from a host of coaches and hangers-on to forsake all other sports and concentrate on 'his game.' "* In other words, Brown would have been recruited by the local "travel team" experts and encouraged to give up that football career. Once again we are not going to go back and there is no doubt that a Jim Brown has been lost over the last 20 years. So let's go forward and implement the Agony of Winning **Strategies.**

Strategy Five: Overcoming the Pressure to Succeed is designed to eliminate distractions and provide the kind of in-the-zone energy that is required to compete in the high-stress, high-pressure atmosphere of today's world of athletics. We are not going to go back to giving kids down time during the summer months. That is a sad fact. In addition, I do not anticipate a retro attitude that says a player SHOULD NOT SPECIALIZE in just one sport and go back to playing multiple sports. I am a realist in that sense. These are very practical **Strategies** that can be used by coaches, players, and parents to understand the components of competing from a place of spirit and joy rather than expectation and agony. The focus of this **Strategy Five: Overcoming the Pressure to Succeed** is to examine the feelings of the participants involved and identify the distractions that a parent, coach, or athlete lives with so we can eliminate them. This strategy continues to promote a level of self-awareness that provides the foundation for focus, concentration, motivation, and commitment that enhances the experience for all those involved with sports. The ability of the participant to either manage or mismanage energy is the determining factor in breaking through to a place where freedom, spirit, and integrity can be enjoyed in the world of sport.

When the parent, coach, or athlete has the tenets of this strategy in working order, they will be able to transform debilitating negative energy to positive energy in real time. It takes much more energy to process negative emotions than positive ones. The system will teach athletes how their distractions affect the quality of their motivation. The lesson will teach athletes about the energy drains that result from carrying around a negative views of coaches, parents, teammates, and themselves.

By becoming aware of distractions, one can recognize negative energy and transform it into powerful responses that develop strength, power, and greatness. It is imperative for athletes, parents, and coaches to operate from a place of positive energy because it is impossible for anyone involved with a negative system of motivation to participate with freedom, spirit, and integrity for long. The athlete may still succeed because skill sometimes overcomes negative energy; however, his or her enjoyment level and feelings of true excellence are greatly diminished.

I like this quote from LGE Performance literature I came across while conducting research for the book. By identifying the distractions and negative feelings that come along with them, we can use positive feelings to transform them and move to a different performance level – to an athletic experience in which the successes can be fully enjoyed.

"... We reach our highest potential when we are connected to our most positive emotional states. Research shows that emotional states such as appreciation, peace, joy, gratitude and love create the biological state of peak

performance. In this state we are relaxed, focused, confident and internally balanced. We are absorbed in the process with no energy invested in the outcome."

These are the exact benefits that completing the Agony of Winning **Strategy Five: Overcoming the Pressure to Succeed** provides for participants in athletic competition.

~~~~~~~~

Concept for Transforming the Agony of Winning to the Thrill of Winning:

It is important to remember that athletes, coaches, and parents are dedicating a lot of time and effort in the never-ending season. That requires us to pay attention to the energy level needed. Be certain to take the time to properly replenish energy by taking time to step away from the sport and not over train.

~~~~~~~~

Question for Transforming the Agony of Winning to the Thrill of Winning:

Why is there so much fear that if some time is spent away from training and playing it would be so detrimental? The truth is that proper rest and a break from the regimen would be beneficial.

~~~~~~~~

Word for Transforming the Agony of Winning to the Thrill of Winning:

Rest

11

Spiritual Relationships In Sports

So many parents enroll their children in sports with the hope that they will attain a scholarship one day. The specialization of one-sport training has given rise to the expectation that it may lead to an education paid in full by the college athletic department. The faster than lightning world in which we live has hastened the world of recruiting. As this process quickens, it works its way down to younger and younger athletes. All semblances of common sense and a level-headed approach to the process have been lost – at quantum speed. The cost to the student/athlete is truly a crime inflicted upon them by adults. The fun of playing, the relationships, and team-oriented outcomes of preparation are no longer a point of emphasis. These elements of participation are the most vital reason to reorient the direction in which sports is headed.

In February 2009, a newspaper in Philadelphia ran the following headline, *"Quarles can't forget his former school."* The well-written article by Phil Anastasia of the *Philadelphia Inquirer* described a South Jersey basketball star, Daryus Quarles, who left his hometown high school basketball team to transfer to *"... a program that plays a national schedule and features several other Division 1 caliber athletes."* Quarles was sold a bill of goods, that going to this high-profile basketball factory, which is basically a basketball recruiting showcase disguised as an educational institution, would enhance his college scholarship chances. The adults in charge did not point out to Quarles that the summers he gave up to attend basketball recruiting factories called basketball camps had already done the job. St. Joseph's Coach Phil Martelli was already recruiting him when he was at his hometown high school, Paulsboro. *"They've been following me since the summer of my freshmen year,"* Quarles said.

The adults guiding this young man failed to point out that the relationships he had with his boyhood friends, in addition to playing for and representing the high school he had dreamed of playing for as a youngster, were valuable considerations. *"I miss Paulsboro,"* Quarles said. *"I try not to watch too much because I want to be out there."* You see, going to Life Center Academy required him to live with other players and the coach, across the street from Life Center. He stayed there during the week and returned home for the weekends. The article pointed out that, *"He attended several Red Raiders ("*

Paulsboro) games, although he said, 'It was tough to sit in the stands and watch his old team without pangs of regret.' "

This situation is not an everyday occurrence for most athletes. However, many parents and athletes read articles like this all the time. The message is clear – give up the things that really matter in sports to enhance your own chances of getting a scholarship. This young man gave up the fun of playing high school ball with his friends. He gave up valuable relationship-building lessons to go on stage at a make-believe school to enhance his chance at a scholarship. This message is not lost on the less talented player who ends up playing a lower level of college basketball. The message being taught is to do what is important to your own personal advancement. I can almost hear the parents telling their children, *"See what this young man did to enhance his career? What do you mean you want to go to the beach with your friends? Now get in the car; it is a two-hour ride to Timbuktu and you have 8 games to play this weekend. Do you think I like doing this every weekend? I have a life too, you know."* This kind of message is filtering down to every ego-driven parent in America. They are ruining the sports playing experience of their children. Believe me, it is an epidemic. **Strategy Six** is **Establishing a Systems of Core Values.** This **Strategy** will guide decision-making for players, parents, and coaches in the increasingly difficult landscape of athletic competition. One of the major **Core Values** in anyone's life should be to establish loving relationships. In my mind and in my experience there is no greater platform to launch lessons teaching the value of loving relationships than participation in athletics.

The most prolific **Core Value** that **Strategy Six: Establishing a Systems of Core Values** incorporates is **Love.** I ran across an article in *Parade* magazine about Joe Ehrmann, a former NFL star, and the high school team he coaches, Gilman High School. He is a volunteer coach. I decided to call Ehrmann and had a nice conversation about his approach to coaching. He reinforced what I read in the article and from a book titled *Season of Life.* Both the article and book were written by Jeffrey Marx who writes that before a game, while giving the team the pregame talk, Ehrmann, *"hobbled into the locker room, with white hair and gold-rimmed glasses. Still, is a mountain of a man. Ehrmann does not need a whistle."* Marx writes that this rather large man skips the usual prep game rah, rah speech and shouts to the team instead, *"What is our job as coaches?"* The team responds with enthusiasm, *"To love us."* Ehrmann shouts back to the team, *"What is your job?"* The boys shout back, *"To love each other!"* Yes, sports fans, this is football we are talking about, that rough and tumble sport that separates the men from the boys. However, let me be clear this exercise is applicable to mens' and womens' sports of all shapes and sizes. The womens' teams I work with can tell you that this particular emotion is as lacking with them as it is with their male counterparts. Athletics, in a very unique and powerful way, has the potential to show the way to compete with care, concern, and compassion for all participants. Then we can send the leaders, trained in these tenets, out into the world to lead with vigor in a more principled manner than the one we see in the world today. The focus of Ehrmann's program is to teach men to be better people; however, the message is applicable to both genders. Once again, he has not sacrificed winning for competing from a place of loving relationships. The Gilman Greyhounds football team in Baltimore is a highly successful program.

The program is committed to being sure that its participants are provided lessons that have nothing to do with winning or losing. As Marx writes, they take the time to *"...stress that Gilman football is all about living in a community. It is about fostering relationships. It is about learning the importance of serving others. While coaches elsewhere scream endlessly about being tough, Ehrmann and Head Football Coach Poggi teach concepts such as empathy, inclusion, and integrity. They emphasize Ehrmann's code of conduct for manhood: accepting responsibility, leading courageously, enacting justice on the behalf of others."*

There is a whole generation of athletes like Daryus Quarles who are missing out on the spiritual relationships that can be developed through athletic participation. I would like to share my most profound experience in relation to developing spiritual relationships through the mechanism of athletic competition.

I wrote about one of the finest student/athletes I have ever had in my Agony of Winning workshops for leadership development. That athlete is Chris LaPierre. Following is another excerpt from the Agony of Winning forum at which he spoke. In his words we can see the intent of his motivation to honor his spiritual relationship with his teammates:

> *"I mentioned earlier that sports should be more than what the scoreboard reads at the end of a game. Along those same lines come personal statistics. A young athlete shouldn't judge how fun a sport is by how good he or she is at it. I'm sure some of you have heard that this past football season I set a few state records, most notably most touchdowns in a season. One thing we*

always talked about was that the accomplishments that I was achieving were not due to my ability, but rather, the work of the other ten guys on the field. We as a team set state records. And we as a team won the championship. Too much emphasis is put on personal accolades."

In his comment here we see that LaPierre and his teammates had a relationship that included discussions about his achievements. He says they always talked about it being a team effort. He was assuring his teammates that he appreciated their relationship and their contribution to his astounding success. This demonstrates the development of a spiritual relationship between the players. He continued:

"A great example came just a few months ago right at the end of our season when the press released the All-County teams and different teams along those lines. And despite having what I repeatedly called the best offensive line in South Jersey, we had zero linemen selected to one of those teams. Now how can they sit there and not recognize any lineman from a back to back state championship team as the best around? I brought it up to a few of the guys after the teams were released and to my surprise, it didn't bother them one bit."

In turn, his teammates told Chris they valued their work as offensive linemen in a relationship with one another that was represented in their being an unselfish unit. They said their success was as a collective whole and their role contributed to his success. That was enough for them. Inside **Strategy Six** in the Agony of Winning system: **Establishing a System**

of Core Values, the team value of **Contribution** is a central theme. This group of Shawnee High School workshop participants certainly applied that lesson in a practical manner. LaPierre finished making his point:

> *"Their point was that the best offensive lines are always recognized as a unit rather than individuals, and they felt honored that I received a lot of accolades, because like I said before, we as a team set those records, and we as a team won the championship. It was great to be part of a team that stressed team accomplishments way before those of individuals, and you can only hope that more young kids grow up with that mindset."*

Now back to the story of Daryus Quarles. Head basketball Coach Phil Martelli at St. Joseph's is one of the really good guys of college coaching. He stresses the life-enhancing lessons that competition offers. What he will get in Daryus Quarles is a great young man taught by adults that the team is secondary to his own advancement. That lesson is the overriding theme of his high school playing experience. His job as a coach who teaches athletics from a proper perspective might have been easier if the adults had been more concerned with Quarles than themselves. Philadelphia Inquirer reporter Phil Anastasia went on in the article to describe the rivalry with Woodbury High School that Quarles missed. *"I would love to play against those guys,"* Quarles said. The Anastasia article brilliantly captures the angst of this prime-time player." Quarles said, *"If I was there, I think we could win it all."* Anastasia continued, *"The gym was overflowing with people an hour before tip-off, unlike his big time game with big-time athletes with no connection with each other competing in an arena with a capacity of 9,000 instead of 1,000 at Paulsboro. However, the big-time arena held no excitement, no fans and cheerleaders doing chants across the crowded gym. Instead you could hear the spirit deadening echoes of the bouncing ball in the atmosphere free building with perhaps 300 curious on lookers in the 9,000-seat arena."* This young man missed out on the relationship-building aspects of being part of the team.

I believe **Strategy Six: Establishing a System of Core Values** is the key to restoring the Thrill of Winning in the world of athletics.

When you know what your values are and live by them, you build strong decision-making skills. Our values are a powerful force guiding the direction we take in life. If you are not in touch with your true values, it is difficult to build self-esteem and maintain long-term happiness. If decision-making is difficult for you and solutions to life's problems seem unclear, you probably do not know what is important to you in those situations. A strong personal foundation and life fulfillment can be achieved through value clarification.

Personal power is obtained by living your values. Having a philosophy and taking actions based on this philosophy provide you with a sense of certainty, an inner peace, and a powerful inner strength. It is important that you set goals that reflect your true values. If you are setting and achieving goals that are not based on what you really want to accomplish in your life, you may feel unfulfilled. A "whatever" attitude sets in.

When you identify your core values and begin to live by them, you can reach the deepest level of personal fulfillment. Most people are not clear on what is truly important to them. Because almost every life decision is guided by our values, it is imperative to identify yours. Your personal power, your self-esteem, your ability to build a strong personal foundation is derived from the skill of having your life values and life actions in agreement.

There is a tremendous power in living your life by your highest ideals. Inner peace, long-range happiness, and a sense of certain direction result from knowing what is important in your life.

~~~~~~~~~

Concept for Transforming the Agony of Winning to the Thrill of Winning:

It is imperative to have a set of Core Values to guide the athletic experience. The most powerful Core Value is love, love of competition and love of practice, games, coaches, opponents, and teammates.

~~~~~~~~~

Question for Transforming the Agony of Winning to the Thrill of Winning:

What Core Value would you add to make your athletic experience more meaningful?

~~~~~~~~~

Word for Transforming the Agony of Winning to the Thrill of Winning:

Love

12

There is an "I" in Team

One of the slogans that coaches use a lot, supposedly to teach that contributing to the team is more noble than individual accomplishment, is *"There is no "I" in the word team."* Like most of the slogans I see on T-shirts and locker room walls, in many instances it is an empty slogan. When a team incorporates the **Strategies** in this book, the coaches will use the time allotted to the "who" aspects of the Agony of Winning system in a way that teaches the meaning behind the slogans posted in locker rooms. The coaches and players will know what the T-shirt messages mean. They will then proceed to incorporate a system of accountability so that the entire program is responsible for maintaining the **Integrity** of that meaning in their actions and behaviors. **Strategy Six:**

Establishing a System of Core Values includes the tenet of personal responsibility, the subject of this chapter, along with the "I" in team and what that means today.

When I spoke with former NFL All-Pro wide receiver Fred Barnett while working on the book, he lamented the loss of camaraderie on the professional level. He told me that 20 years ago in the pro locker room there were closer relationships and friendships than there are in the locker room today. "Kevin, we did things off the field together," he said. "We went bowling; we went to each other's houses, in large groups. We hung around in the locker room after practice and were part of each other's lives." I could sense his sadness over what he sees as a bygone era. Barnett continued, "Today you walk into the locker room and it is like there are 40 different individual corporations instead of 40 players comprising a team. Everyone has an administrative assistant and an entourage of 'helpers' hanging around. The team feels like it contains 40 different teams within a team." It sounds as if he was saying there are a lot of individuals and no team concept.

Of course, I haven't seen any administrative assistants on the high school or college level yet; however, the deep personal relationships are not as fully developed as they once were on those levels either. There is a very limited perception outside of what may benefit the individual's career. The message inherent in this long cherished motto used by coaches for eons is that there is no room for selfish individuals on the team; therefore, no "I" in the word team. I have a little different slant on the slogan. I feel more than ever that the individual or the "I" in the team needs to be emphasized more. The principles of **Strategy Six: Establishing a System of Core Values** need to be taught to every player in every program in America. And each "I" on the team needs to embrace the principles so the "we" – the team as a unit – may benefit from the individuals' personal growth. The particular **Core Value of Self Responsibility** holds the potential for the athletes to learn that they will be held responsible for behavior that demonstrates their commitment to the whole.

It is challenging to cultivate an attitude within the athlete that the team is first and their individual success is second, given the culture of athletics today. Especially when the emphasis on the individualized, specialized training is geared toward that one player's results and not how it will benefit the whole. For instance, when was the last time you were at a specialized training center and heard a parent say, "Joanie is really giving it her all in these sessions. It is very expensive, but it will all be worth it if the team is better off as a result of our personal sacrifice." All I can say is keep searching if you have not heard that yet.

For sure, in my own playing career, I wanted to get better as an individual when I spent my summers on the hot asphalt of Crescent Field playing for hours on end. However, the overriding goal for all of us was to get better so that collectively we could make Dover High School the Conference Champs. I remember one thing very clearly about one of the fathers who sometimes came and watched us work out at the court. He was the father of my best friend, Danny Benz, and he was always encouraging all of us to be better, not just his son. I knew he genuinely wanted to see me get along better with Danny, simply because we were friends, teammates, and so the basketball team could reach new heights.

Today's parents operate from a fear that their child is not going to get "theirs." My father had that mind-set so I can recognize it a mile away. Shari Kuchenbecker, a California research psychologist and author of the book <u>Raising Winners: A Parent's Guide to Helping Kids Succeed On and Off the Playing Field</u>, believes part of the problem lies in the changing dynamics of families. She says she sees some parents overindulging kids, which may create me-first attitudes and lead to emphasis on winning by any means. "So many of our kids are growing up feeling entitled, and they're brats," she says. It is impossible for Junior not to feel like he is "all that" when the parent is either gushing all over him or pushing him to accomplish individual goals. This is one reason why there is definitely an "I" in team. That "I" stands for me, me, and me. A new kind of "I" needs to be established, an "I" that means the Agony of Winning **Strategies** will be established with each "I" on the team so they will all understand there is no "I" in TEAM.

One of the **Core Values** taught in **Strategy Six** is **Personal Sacrifice**. In today's sports world often times personal sacrifice means personal gain. If the team should do better as a byproduct of personal gain then that's great, but that is not the primary goal in a lot of cases. It is imperative that coaches adopt **Strategy One** and make sure time is allotted to nurture an attitude of contribution to the whole and that there actually is a bigger whole the athlete is responsible to. This means the success of the team is the bigger goal, not individual success. The paradox lies in the fact that the "I" – the individual player – needs to be developed fully so that contribution to the whole becomes a driving force for the individual.

That attitude needs to be nurtured and developed, just like a set of muscles. One of the reasons athletic programs do not have this kind of teaching as a priority goes back to what I pointed out in my discussion of **Strategy One**. If 95% of the contact time allotted for preparation in sports is used to hone the technical skill side of "what" to do, or the physical side, there is little time left to explore the depth of the slogan. The sports delivery system rarely, if ever, scratches below the surface of the inspirational quotes it provides athletes. We are cheating the athletes, coaches, and parents by not teaching these lessons, lessons that used to come a bit more naturally.

As I pointed out in previous chapters, I was hired by two very different high school football coaches, Coach Mehigan at Cherokee High School and Coach Gushue at Shawnee High School. Coach Mehigan is a relatively young head football coach and Coach Gushue has coached for 30 years. Both coaches however, wanted the same results from my work with their teams. They wanted me to work with their players on developing, leadership, motivation, and inspiration by implementing the Agony of Winning Strategies. I know they hired me because they are good men who wanted to help their players develop as men. They are very competitive and want to win, but it is easy to see they are also coaches who want to develop the character of the young people under their tutelage.

Coaches P.J. Mehigan and Tim Gushue were already on the fringe of applying some tenets of the Agony of Winning **Strategies** before I went to work for them. They knew they needed to allot time to the behavioral and attitudinal aspects of their programs, if they were going to do more than just win football games. Even though they were already doing some work in this area they were humble enough to know that a professional like me, with expertise in the area of personal growth and development, might be able to complement and supplement what they were already doing.

Coaches Gushue and Mehigan are the epitome of the slogan that there is no "I" in team. They were not concerned about "outsourcing" their motivational duties to another. I had a coach with a very limited perspective say to me once that he was in charge of motivating his players. The paradox here is that coach knew he had to improve in this area to help his team grow on a personal level. He knew that ultimately my system would make winning less of an agony and more of a thrill. But he worried about what others would say if he "outsourced" that part of his job. So in the case of Coaches Gushue and Mehigan they know that there is an "I" in Team. For them the "I" in team means their own willingness to be responsible for personal growth so they could look at sports from a broader perspective. By placing "I" back in team they were taking personal responsibility to grow as individuals and enhance their passion for the **Intrinsic** portions of athletic competition. This story is the fundamental concept, that there is an "I" in team but not in the way most people think about. We need to alter the system for the delivery of the full potential of athletics by growing the "I" first, and then we can take it back out. This way there is an "I" in team until the participants understand that it is really not about them as individuals but the whole. We need this attitude now more than ever.

If coaches are only spending 3 to 5% of practice time on behavior and attitude they are doing the teaching of life lessons in athletics a disservice. In fact, currently the only time allotment in most athletic programs for intrinsic personal growth lessons is used to research and print out the motivational statements and quotes that are not being fully explored. We are left with a reactionary approach to making sure the coach and athlete live up to the standard of behavior and attitude required by the slogans. For example, if a coach detects some selfish behavior by a player, they make a comment or make an example of that player, maybe even punishing him. There are very few pre-emptive active approaches to teaching, setting goals, and then establishing a system of accountability to the standard inherent in the slogan "There is no "I" in team." There isn't time for that stuff, a lot of coaches tell me. So they post signs and make T-shirts.

There is an "I" in team because the team is composed of a collection of individuals. The strength of the team as a whole is directly related to the personal foundation and integrity of each individual. Personal **Integrity** is a foundational concept in **Strategy Four: Code of Ethics: Setting a Tone for Integrity, Respect, and Civility**. The old slogan about the weakest link breaking the chain under pressure applies here. Once again, there is an "I" in team until the integrity of each person is strong enough to contribute to the whole. It should be noted right here that a team with superior technical skills can overcome a lack of behavioral and attitudinal integrity and still be successful and win. However, there is a huge difference in setting out with an intention of just being good in terms of wins and losses and being excellent in terms of providing a platform for the personal growth of coaches, players, and parents.

I once worked for the Ridge High School Football Team in New Jersey. The team I worked with and the team from the season before I conducted the Agony of Winning workshop, had the same record in terms of wins and losses. So their success level as measured by the outside world – the extrinsic measurement – was not altered by my establishment of the **Strategies of** the Agony of Winning within the program. There was, however, a huge shift in the unselfish nature of the team I worked with because of the adoption of the Agony of Winning **Strategy Two.** In addition, the **Core Value** of **Personal Sacrifice** made the experience of being a team member more enjoyable. The spirit of sport was internalized by the players and some of the coaches so that success (external) was more satisfying because of the way the players challenged their behavior and attitude (internal).

Essentially, there are two different types of "I" in team. One particular team suffered from having just one star player inflicted with the kind of "I" that gave birth to the original slogan. They had a player who was ego-driven and only concerned about her own statistics. They had the kind of player who would rather play a great individual game even if the team lost. That scenario was more desirable to that player than if she had played a so-so game but the team won. Having a player operate with this kind of "I" drained the team of having a joyful playing experience despite the fact the team had a great win-loss record. The positive energetic state of a successful team was compromised by a selfish yet talented player.

However, a year later a different "I" was prevalent on the team. Through the **Strategies** I am presenting in this book, we established an "I" that was rooted in the players taking personal responsibility for not only improving their technical skills, but their behavior.

Coach Tom Falato sent me a note about the Agony of Winning **Strategies.** "This program fundamentally changed the way I communicate with players. The leaders show a tremendous sense of putting the team first even in the most difficult part of the season. Wow what a program."

Another team I worked with had a player who exemplified the promise of personal growth for all athletes who put the proper "I" in team. This young man, Jeff Maccarella, was slated to be the team's quarterback going into his senior year, however, the coaching staff had other ideas. They thought the team as a whole would benefit more if they moved this young man to defense to play cornerback and placed a talented junior in his place as quarterback. Although it was a hard transition, he changed position for the betterment of the team. Through the work in our sessions, he was able to adopt the "I" in team that comes with personal sacrifice for the good of the whole. He sent an e-mail to me about the impact of the program and how it helped him put his situation in the proper perspective. He moved positions his senior year and put the "I" on hold for the betterment of the team. In his email he wrote,

"I have found myself not looking at the move so negatively. I find myself more upbeat, even during the day at school. The Agony of Winning program has already helped me be a better person."

I work in several high school and college programs where the coaches have decided it is important that each player become a better person through behavior and attitude enhancement. They have hired me to build their teams on the inside, so that it enhances what happens on the outside. These coaches have sat in on the training. There is no question that the manner in which the team as a whole performs their technical skills has been enhanced because we put the "I" back in team, the correct "I," which requires the coaches and athletes to look on the inside to rediscover their own spirit and the underlying passion and motivation that propels them to compete. Coaches Tim Gushue and Paula Escadero of Shawnee High School in New Jersey, P.J. Mehigan of Cherokee High School, Tony Farrell of New Egypt, Michele Sharp, Margie Akers and Dan

Garrett of Kean University, Jim Knowles of Cornell University, Rocky Hager of Northeastern University, Kim Bonus of the Wilmoor School of Gymnastics and many other coaches have all deemed it important that their players learn more than how to perform in the gym and on the playing field.

These coaches are motivated to provide a system that values process based athletics, so their players can enhance their personal well-being as well as their physical prowess. They hired me to help change, develop, or enhance the culture of their programs one player at a time. Through my workshops, they hold their players accountable throughout the year to the tenets established in my meetings with the team.

~~~~~~~~~

Concept for Transforming the Agony of Winning to the Thrill of Winning:

There is an "I" in team until each person has as their main motivation a commitment to grow as an individual so the team benefits. Only then is there no more "I" in team.

~~~~~~~~~

Question for Transforming the Agony of Winning to the Thrill of Winning:

Are your attitudes and actions in alignment with the idea of putting the team first and yourself second?

~~~~~~~~~

Word for Transforming the Agony of Winning to the Thrill of Winning:

"I"

13

Handling Disappointment

I remember having a discussion with a parent of a college quarterback that illustrated the fact that parents and players have a hard time handling the disappoint that often comes with athletic competition. In this case the parent was disappointed with the way his son was being handled by the head football coach. Now, mind you, the young man was named starter as a freshman in college and went on to start all four seasons of his college career. The parent was spouting off over the fact that his son was being mishandled by the head coach, and he was going to give the coach a piece of his mind. The tone of his conversation indicated he was not schooled in the principles of **Strategy Four: Code of Ethics: Setting a Tone for Integrity, Respect, and Civility**. I was relatively certain the coach was going to be on the receiving end of that tone.

I pointed out to the parent that the coach must know a little about coaching. This man had won two National Championships on the college level and was noted in the coaching industry as a man of tremendous character who helped mold young men. The parent countered by citing his own coaching credentials, they were very impressive and shut me up in a hurry. The scary thing is he was serious. He told me he had been a player at his son's level of college ball. OK, that helps me understand that he at least knows the rubs of football. However, what he was really hanging his hat on was that he had been a midget football coach in the community for years. HE WAS A MIDGET FOOTBALL COACH? PLEASE!

The least trained of all coaches in the entire country are youth coaches. This man believed that because he played on the college level and coached 10-year-olds, his knowledge base and ability to "run" a program rivaled that of the head coach at the college level. In fact, Joel Fish of the Center for Sports Psychology in Philadelphia writes, *"I am calling on all organizations that administer youth sports to have highly trained professionals oversee the sports programs."*

Engh, president of the National Alliance for Youth Sports, says, *"In most leagues they're volunteers that organize and administer sports for children with usually no education on what this is about, and no accountability to anyone."*

This parent truly believed his credentials warranted a valid opinion; he truly felt that was a fact. Although he is certainly entitled to his opinion, he lacked **Strategy Four: Code of Ethics: Setting a Tone for Integrity, Respect, and Civility** for sure. Even his tone with me during our discussion was uncivil. He had no respect for the coach. I am not suggesting we should blindly hand out respect, but in this case, the head coach had earned that respect over a career that spanned thirty years. The real problem was that the team was not winning. That was it in a nut shell.

This young man and his family had met with nothing but success up until this point in his career. He was now the quarterback on a team with a losing record. Once again, if all the value derived from athletic competition is based on winning and losing, we are throwing away some valuable lessons. **Strategy Two: Competing with Purpose and Passion** would have been helpful for this family. There were many lessons about the value of setting **Intrinsic Goals** inherent in this situation, which can be derived from **Strategy Three: Maintaining a Balance of Intrinsic and Extrinsic Goals**

It is imperative that we identify and teach the **Agony of Winning Strategy Six: Establishing a System of Core Values** to parents/fans, coaches, and athletes alike. No less than three or four Agony of Winning **Strategies** could be applied to this family's situation. In sports today we are facing parental abuse of young athletes as well as verbal abuse heaped on coaches from the bleachers. It is time to incorporate and mandate ethical practices and a set of core values so we can change this.

Parents seem to have trouble holding their children accountable. If a player has experienced frustration with a coach, a large majority of parents, armed with ESPN-fueled expert knowledge of the game, immediately point the finger, yes, sometimes *that* finger, at the coach. After all, can't those coaches see the value of little Joanie/Johnny being the star of the team? I think parents have lost the ability to let their kids fail. They fail themselves to see the value in the athlete learning to handle and manage disappointment. This is a very valuable life lesson that sports has the potential to teach. There is a big upside in "failing," in losing, in being disappointed. I know in my own life "failing," or just not getting the starting job, or being a second team All-Star instead of first team, which I thought I deserved, taught me to persevere. The contrast of "failing" or feeling disappointed provides an opportunity for everyone involved to experience the feeling of succeeding more intensely. In addition, the establishment of a system for the **Core Values** of **Appreciation, Gratitude and Perseverance** for ALL the experiences that participation can provide for coaches, parents, and athletes is sometimes most prevalent in the perceived failures.

In one Southern New Jersey town a family actually sued the Board of Education over the fact that their son was cut from the basketball team. The mother was a school board member to boot and had to resign so she wasn't suing herself. In the lawsuit she contended that her son suffered emotional distress. Yeah, no kidding. There are some feelings of disappointment when someone does not achieve a goal they set. If her son was suffering I would say that his inability to handle disappointment and perhaps his own sense of entitlement needed to be investigated, rather than the initiation of a lawsuit.

I am sure that Michael Jordan suffered some emotional distress when he was cut from the varsity team in high school when he was a sophomore. However, he did not sue the school board. Instead, being cut, or "failing," provided him with the opportunity of a lifetime. This situation presented the entire family with the opportunity to adopt the Agony of Winning **Core Values** of **Resilience and Commitment** to getting better. Being cut pushed Jordan to tap into an intrinsic awareness that not being cut might not have provided him with. He found a spot inside himself to push himself to perfect his game. As he later stated, *"I think that not making the varsity team drove me to really work at my game, and also taught me that if you set goals, and work hard to achieve them, the hard work can pay off."*

The lawsuit also claimed that the woman's teen chances for a college scholarship were diminished because he was cut from the team. I am not trying to say coaches are always right, far from it. However, I can tell you that coaches love to win. In fact, a lot of coaches put their own value system on hold when it comes to winning. I can assure you that this coach was not going to cut a scholarship-caliber athlete based on any personal vendetta he held against him or the family. If the kid could help him win the state title he would put up with an uncomfortable relationship.

These parents essentially robbed this young man of the opportunity for personal growth. They could have used the fact that he got cut to its larger potential for teaching life lessons. They could have taught him that we do not always get the outcome we desire in life and that despite our earnest effort and hard work the outcomes we want do not materialize every time. The hard facts are that sometimes life is just not fair. The athlete's positive response to disappointment is one of the character qualities that participating in athletics can provide. It is the adult's responsibility to teach that. I agree with Bob Behre, who is the author of a well know sports blog when he writes, *"Our society has become possessed with protecting our kids from failure. Failure is good."* I know what he means.

In today's world, in general, and in sports specifically, we try to shield players and parents from disappointment. We are robbing them of a very rich experience. There is a difference between civility in dealings with parents and the level of political correctness that is robbing coaches from being honest about children's playing capabilities. One must be careful with his or words today. It is the same with players. They do not see the value in being disappointed. It is their responsibility to process it and grow from their experiences.

This story is worth telling because it fits so nicely into this discussion. It is about someone who was there to teach me a lesson about how to counteract disappointment. No, not my father, that person was my sister Maureen. My dear sister provided me with a lesson many parents are cheating their children out of today. A lot of principles of the Agony of Winning **Strategies** that I have developed were arrived at through experiences in my own life.

Preceding my junior year in high school I set out on a personal training program that would help me become a great high school basketball player. I wanted to be one of the best in the whole Lakeland area, as it was referred to back in the late 1960s. I practiced my skills religiously. The fruits of my practicing every day that summer at Crescent Field in south Dover were about to be demonstrated in blazing August heat at the Basketball Camp of the Lakers. In the first two days of camp, it was evident I was not the same player who had ended the season last March. I was no longer the player who did not even start on the J.V. team. My improvement was nothing short of dramatic and miraculous. It is important to note that I did set **Extrinsic Goals** for myself as subscribed to in the Agony of Winning **Strategies**. **Extrinsic Goals** are important, they give us direction, a road map if you will as to where we are headed. However, the most important factor in my dramatic improvement was the spiritual and passionate intentions I possessed in my soul to accomplish this goal. As I trained, I was in touch with a glee I felt when I played basketball. In this story I was putting into action the principles that would later be developed into the Agony of Winning **Strategy Two: Competing with Purpose and Passion.**

The coaches' appreciation did not go unnoticed. You see, the coaches thought they were recognizing this relentless, hard working, hustling player. *"He gets the most out of his ability," they said. "A real hustler is that kid Kevin Touhey. He treats every drill, every play in the game as if it is his last."* What was really happening was my absolute connection to the spirit of sports, the spirit of competing against oneself. The "why" of the Agony of Winning triangle was fully operational and providing that inner fire I had for competing.

The first day of camp I played the best basketball I had ever played. The second day I topped that. While I cleaned the tables in the cafeteria after dinner that second day, Coach Luciano, the varsity coach at Dover High School, came up to see me. He congratulated me on my play the first two days of camp and encouraged me to keep up the good work. I assured him I would. As he was ready to step away from me, he said that if I did keep getting better he was going to have a hard time keeping me out of the line-up. I was on cloud nine.

My confidence soared. Each day I worked harder and played better than the day before. On the third day of camp, I was chosen for the coaches' award, which signified hustle and improvement. I had my picture taken with the trophy. It was my first basketball trophy. Coach Luciano commented that

I was really going to make it hard for him not to choose me over the players it was assumed would be starters that coming season. That fall I worked even harder at Crescent Field courts to improve my game. I would go to the court before everyone else arrived and play make up games of every kind to assure my spot in the line-up on opening day.

When it was time to go home, I would dribble home at full speed up the steep hill my family lived on. Crescent Field was on Second Street. My house was straight up the hill right after Sixth Street. The very last game I would play would be to dribble up the hill between the fallen leaves. The object was to avoid hitting any leaves with the ball. If I hit a leaf while dribbling I had to go back a street and start again. Some nights it took me a long time to dribble home.

That fall I was full of confidence and optimism that I would be a starter. I had been securely attached to the expectation that I would be a starter based on the summer camp and the early workouts. That was until the pre-season news articles about the team came out. They were of course touting, and rightly so, returning starters Craig Schiffner and Frank Bassense. In addition, Danny and Mike Gruber were featured as potential stars who had played some as sophomores, and they should have been. Many other players were mentioned including an up and coming sophomore named Ray DiLorenzo. I was way down the list, mentioned as an afterthought in the article.

I read the article and told myself the writers did not understand how much I improved, but surely Coach knew. The writers would soon see the errors of their ways. They will certainly be surprised. Well, I was the one who was in for a surprise. Until my best friend Danny Benz got sick in late December, I was not in the starting line-up. I sat on the bench for the first six games of the season. Sometimes, I hardly played in the games at all. The coach did not trust that what he had seen in the summer and practice was enough to get me in the games. With all due respect to Coach, even though I was undersized for that position, I knew I was one of the best five players in the program and should have been on the court from the start of the season.

My sister Maureen became my biggest supporter during this period. She has told me she admired my **persistence**. That **Core Value** of mine was the only thing keeping me going. That and the "why" of my competing, which was the absolute inner desire and love I had for basketball. She told me that eventually the coach would see that, too. I had her positive support, not support based on bashing the coach as an imbecile who could not discern how vital to the team I was. Maureen, of course, without knowing it, was modeling for me the principles adhered to in **Strategy Four: Code of Ethics: Setting a Tone for Integrity, Respect, and Civility.** Her remarks were always centered on what I could do, not what Coach wasn't doing. She provided me with a spiritual resilience that I drew on every day. I was sad and disappointed, but I hung in there. I didn't seek legal action against Coach Luciano for poor judgment detrimental to an adolescent athlete.

Maureen would talk to me for hours about not conceding, not giving up. She never once provided me with an out by being critical of Coach. She purchased a book about Bill Bradley titled *"A Sense of Where You Are"* for me to read, which provided inspiration. I read it from cover to cover. The book covered the period before Bradley was a basketball star at Princeton University. The book detailed the training and techniques that made Bradley the extraordinary athlete he became. But athletic prowess alone would not explain Bradley's magnetism, which is in the quality of the man himself – his self-discipline, his rationality, and his sense of responsibility. She provided me with tools, not excuses. I turned the pages of that book thousands of times and became more inspired each time. I kept playing hard in practice every day. Every night I came home to hear my father yell about how the coach did not like me and I would never get in the line-up. It all came to a head preceding our game against Morris Catholic High School.

All my old friends from Sacred Heart School in Dover where I went from grades 5 through 8, who went to Morris Catholic, would be there. It was very important to me to play a lot in this game, even if I was not going to start. The gym was packed, and many of my old friends were present. As I warmed up, I stayed focused on the hope that once I got in the game I would play so well Coach would not be able to take me out. That hope was based on how excellent I practiced that week. I remember it so clearly. The result or outcome of that effort was one insignificant minute of playing time during the entire game. I was devastated. My whole family was at the game. My father left in disgust. Maureen stayed to drive me home after the game.

The minute I sat in the front seat I started to cry – hard. The tears were flushing my self-esteem and confidence away with them. I can see and hear Maureen encouraging me not to give up. I could feel her energy as she prodded me not to forget the message from the Bill Bradley book. She was very loving toward me. As my self-esteem streamed down my cheeks, I thought about what more I could do to get playing time. What would I say at the lunch table about why I did not play more? How would I handle my father when I got home? My confidence was shattered. The bright lights of appreciation that had shown on me during the Lakers' summer camp experience were dimmed to a single notch in a deep, dark cavern. My commitment to the self-imposed principles inside the Agony of Winning **Strategy Two: Competing with Purpose and Passion** was being challenged in a big way. To my father, there was not much emphasis on the value of the training I engaged in before the season to ensure my success. It was only the outcome that mattered. Because my career was, up to this point anyway, not reaping the deserved outcome, I felt unappreciated in my household and embarrassed at school.

However, armed with the Agony of Winning system of setting **Intrinsic** goals, I continued to love the whole idea of athletic competition. I loved to practice. I loved training, and I loved my friends as much as a teammate could love another teammate. So after the game and the post-game barrage from my father, I retreated to the sanctuary of my heart and soul, which housed my love of sports, my love of the art of competition.

In my bed, I reconnected with my own true nature. As I listened to my transistor radio close to my ear, I tapped into that spiritual connection and drew strength from it. If you are aware of your own identity during the process, the richness of the experience is not lost even if the outcome is not arrived at. Even if not truly appreciated by others I could look myself in the mirror of true value-based integrity. I told myself I would do my best tomorrow regardless of whether my **Extrinsic** goal of starting happened.

I kept improving in practice. I ran circles around the first team. Then my best friend, no coincidence, went down with illness and I was in the starting line-up for the first conference game. The long-awaited outcome of all my training had arrived. I played like my life depended on it, which it did. Michael said to me, "Relax, Kevin, you will be all right in your first varsity start." I told Mike he did not have to worry. I carried over what I had done in practice and ran circles around Jefferson. I played so well Coach Luciano had no choice but to bench Mike Harris and move me to his position as a forward when Danny returned for the next game. I never missed another game in the Dover uniform.

I was a powerful force on the team from the time I stepped on the court at Jefferson. I was proud to receive the award as the team's Most Improved Player. Coach had handed me a trophy that was a symbol of my willingness to **persevere.**

Life is full of disappointments. It is imperative that all of us involved with athletics understand that teaching players and parents to learn from disappointment is important to their personal growth. The bumps in the road provided for the participants in sports are great opportunities to show ourselves we have what it takes to overcome the bump.

Concept for Transforming the Agony of Winning to the Thrill of Winning:

Athletics provides a unique opportunity to teach parents, coaches, and players how to handle disappointment. Disappointment is prevalent when participating in sports. It is imperative to learn the life skill of taking the opportunity that disappointment provides us with and handling it with grace and humility.

Question for Transforming the Agony of Winning to the Thrill of Winning:

How do you handle disappointment? Are you quick to blame others or make an excuse or do you take personal responsibility?

Word for Transforming the Agony of Winning to the Thrill of Winning:

Opportunity

14

When Second Place is No Place

When second place is no place and only being No. 1 one counts for anything, we have lost opportunities for the sports experience to be awesome. The drive to crown the one and only champion has over time diminished the awe that each and every practice and game can provide for the participant. The movement in college football to establish a playoff system to ensure we have one champion is gaining momentum. This movement is proof positive that the entire system of athletics is rooted almost exclusively in the value of accomplishing **Extrinsic Goals**. There is an imbalance in athletics when **Intrinsic Goals** are not set. The Agony of Winning **Strategy Two: Competing with Purpose and Passion** is a valuable resource that teaches the benefits of sports that have little to do with winning and losing. One of the principles **Strategy Two** teaches student athletes, parents, and coaches is how to maintain a sense of awe, gratitude, and appreciation for the special nature of their participation in athletics. When second place is no place it becomes difficult to maintain passion over time. The experience of competing becomes mundane.

Alex Rodriguez was quoted as saying, "Now I just have an opportunity to come out and play baseball and have fun." He said this after the New York Yankees won the 2009 World Series. When second place is no place the underlying feeling is not joy but just relief. That is a shame. Rodriguez said, "… a humongous gorilla came off my back." Maybe it was the weight of carrying the second-place-is-no-place gorilla around for his entire career that led to his use of steroids. That is not an excuse but perhaps a reason for the out-of-control nature of competitive sports. I know this is a professional athlete we are talking about, and pro sports is a business. However, young athletes look up to the pros; they pay attention to what they have to say. When the prevailing attitude is that second place is no place, it brings with it "a humongous gorilla." Competing becomes harder for participants to enjoy if they land in any place but first, not to mention last place.

I worked for Northeastern University and their great Head Coach Rocky Hager from 2005 through 2008. They did not have a winning season then. Coach Hager had a predisposition to the Agony of Winning **Strategies** and had employed a variation of them throughout his career. I met him when he was an assistant at Temple University and I was conducting Agony of Winning workshops with the team there. Despite not having a winning team, Coach Hager wanted to make sure the players and coaches got the message that athletics teaches many things other than wins and losses. He wanted them to be aware that they had personal responsibility to something greater than their win/loss record. Coach Hager sent me this e-mail after my first workshop with his team:

> *The players said it was just a great 3 hour program. One of our seniors said you gave the best presentation he has ever heard in his 3 years here. Kevin, the entire program, coaches included, look forward to your return for summer camp.*
>
> *R.E. "Rocky" Hager*
>
> *Head Football Coach*

It is a good thing the players on this team had a coach who felt responsible for establishing the Agony of Winning **Strategy Six: Establishing a System of Core Values.** He wanted them to experience value even thought their record did not indicate they were successful. He also fully embraces the concepts brought forth in ***Strategy Two: Competing with Purpose and Passion.*** He wanted his players to know that a loss did not have to interfere with their **passion** for the game and that there was a deeper **purpose** to their participation in college athletics.

It is necessary to once again point out that what is happening on the professional sports level and the college level trickles down to the lowest levels. I am convinced that we have ESPN coverage of the Little League World Series because of what happens in the major leagues. Yes, I am. When the only emphasis is on being No. 1, when cheating and the steroid use is basically getting endorsed in the media directly and indirectly, it affects younger athletes. You have your head in the sand if you think that some of the young athletes', coaches' and parents' attitudes are not shaped by the media coverage of these stories. I am not endorsing blackballing these stories. I am endorsing incorporating the **Strategies** in this book to give parents, coaches, and players a different angle from which to view the situation and to help shape an attitude with a more compassionate perspective for competing. The Strategies teach that there are ample opportunities to compete with awe, appreciation, and gratitude whether or not we have a playoff system that ensures only one winner.

The headline atop an editorial by one of my favorite *Philadelphia Inquirer* columnists, Michael Smerconish, reads, *"A law to mandate college football playoffs?"* He endorses the idea of a college playoff system, I like him, and many of his views on athletics in America, especially his commentary on the sad state of youth sports. However, I believe his opinion on this issue is really off and based on the idea that Second Place is No Place. It is a bit ironic because Smerconish has written columns in which he laments the loss of the multi-sports athlete and how we are asking young participants to choose a single sport. He writes, *"At the rate we're going, dugouts will need to be lined with high chairs; Gatorade will launch a brand of apple juice. Need new Under Armour? Try Baby Gap."* I agree with his slant on this growing problem. There is a direct correlation between the drive at higher levels of competition to crown one ultimate winner and the fact that we are robbing the youth of America of a chance for having fun with athletic competition. Hence the need for The Agony of Winning **Strategy Two: Competing with Purpose and Passion.**

We are starting children in serious organized sports at too

young an age. This is an adult thing. Parents and youth coaches are always telling me how much the kids love it. Of course 5-, 6- and 7-year-olds are going to love the idea of having uniforms, wrist bands, games with official rules and regulations, referees, a full complement of coaches, and, of course, the ever-present trophy for showing up in uniform for the games. It is cute, after all, to see that little 5-year-old, a couple years removed from a uniform that included diapers, a bib and a pre-game meal of formula and Gerber's split pea delight, in full sports regalia. The challenge is becoming one of competition burnout early in their playing career.

It starts at the top and filters its way down the line. Smerconish is not connecting the dots between the two, so he endorses the idea of Congress getting involved. *"Should Congress be involved in revising college football postseason? Yes is the short answer,"* he writes. I have an even shorter answer, "No." The article states that 85% of college football fans favor changing the current system. Smerconish writes *"...every year at this time, the legions of reporters, observers and fans wishing to move to a single, elimination playoff, like the NFL, for example – take their shots at the Bowl Championship Series (BCS) system."* With all due respect, the very last place I would want to get an unbiased opinion about what should be important to the integrity of athletics is from parents, fans, and the media. Yes sir, if I was looking for some guidance on the college playoff system, I would want to see what the fans think about it before I made a move.

God forbid that we should have 30 or so bowls, like the current system allows for, so some of the Davids of college football can get the feeling of playing in a bowl, just like the Goliaths of college football. Teddy Greenstein, columnist with the *Chicago Tribune,* wrote a piece that speaks to my point, *"Amid all the fun, we have people yelling that the sport has to change. It needs a playoff system. Why? So the casual fans who are confused by the BCS and the angry columnists who write about college football three times a year can get finality."* He continues his point more strongly, *"Great idea. Let's make college football more like the NFL, which would rival rodeo in popularity if it weren't for gambling and fantasy football."*

I believe that when all the emphasis is on the end result in athletics and we continually employ a system that narrows the definition of successful, we lose something from the day-to-day measurements of success. The process, Agony of Winning **Strategy Six: Establishing a System of Core Values** needs to be put into action. Maybe Congress could vote that into the system instead of the playoffs.

Greenstein continues, *"Or better yet, let's have a 16-team playoff as is done in the NBA, where the regular season is so boring the arenas pipe in music during the games and the fans pay full attention only to the 'entertainment' during timeouts. We all love the NCAA basketball tournament. But you can't do it with football. A team can't play six games in 18 days. And let's face it, non-conference basketball games are gloried exhibitions. College football plays meaningful games every Saturday."*

I love the message inherent in what Greenstein writes. I would like to take it a bit further. Every game is important. Every time an athlete practices or plays in a game it is important. Participating in athletic contests and preparing for them carry important lessons. Many of those lessons are provided for in the Agony **of Winning Strategies** presented in this book. That is precisely what the Agony of Winning **Strategy**

Two: Competing with Purpose and Passion teaches, to assign important lessons to athletic participation that go beyond what place you finish in.

In our society we have lost the ability to feel **Awe**. **Strategy Six: Establishing a System of Core Values** includes **Awe** as a **Core Value**. In my workshops, I help participants reconnect to moments that produced for them the feeling of **Awe**. I share with them that in our society we "step over," meaning we do not pay attention to so many important little things that could provide the feeling of **Awe** because we are involved in a quest for the big thing. If you have received 30 trophies "just because" and played thousands of games before reaching high school, it is hard to feel **Appreciation**, **Gratitude**, and **Awe**. So in the world of sports, if nothing changes or gets worse what can we do? We can engage in the process provided by the Agony of Winning **Strategies** to put things in perspective and create awareness. We can teach participants how to pay attention to what is going on, we can urge participants to fall awake, if you will, because everyone is sleep walking through the athletic experience.

I read this on a sports blog once and copied it without getting the author's name. But it is worth sharing, *"My 8 year old is nephew playing little league. His team lost and he was mad about it. I asked him two questions. 1. Did you play the best you could? 'Yeah,' and 2. did you have fun? Another 'yeah,' and I told him those things are what count, doing your (personal) best and enjoying the game. He shook his funk off and decided to go practice throwing and catching."*

I think in youth sports we can start to dispel the idea that second place is no place. Youth sports is the best place to begin restoring a sense of **Awe** to the games we play. We can begin there to replace "second place is no place" with "isn't it Awesome to compete, play and have fun." Consider the following:

This story is about a fifth-grader, Abby Harpenau, whose parents were trying to buy basketball shoes for their daughter to wear for her YMCA basketball team. Abby was hoping they could find girls shoes that she could wear. As much as her parents tried they could not find them because of her shoe size, very large for her age.

I heard about this situation, as I coached her older brother for many years and Debbie and I are friends with the Harpenau family. Abby's mom shared their dilemma with Debbie. I happened to have an extra pair of basketball shoes that we purchased for our Niles Girls' Varsity program that were the exact size Abby needed. When Debbie called Abby's mom to tell her that Coach Touhey was willing to give Abby the same pair of shoes that the Niles Girls' Varsity team wears to play games, Abby was shocked beyond belief. Abby is a big fan and attends most of our high school games. When her mom told her about the shoes, Abby's said to her mom, "You mean the same exact shoe that the high school girls varsity team wears?" Her mom assured her they were the same shoes. Abby could hardly control her excitement.

My wife delivered the shoes and when Abby saw me at the next basketball game she ran to me and gave me the biggest hug. She thanked me and said that she was so lucky to be wearing those shoes. She also assured me that every time she puts those shoes on she would hustle more and play harder than anyone else.

What Abby may never know is that the love she poured out to me was a gift that she gave to me that was much larger than the shoes she received. How wonderful that a high school basketball team could have that kind of impact on a little girl." — *Coach Patrick Touhey.*

My brother told me this story as we discussed how the athletic community as a whole has lost a sense of awe that accompanies the magical world that sports can be. There are so many awesome opportunities to generate good feelings around sports. The **Pressure to Succeed** and an insistence that our young athletes grow up so fast has robbed us of that sense of awe. What is the rush? Why do we have to step over the multitudes of wholesome experiences on our way to the end product?

Youth sports can be the place we start to restore the awe of the athletic experience for the participants. But the fact is that in Little League baseball, 70 percent of the players drop out by age 13. Why? A study conducted by the National Alliance for Youth Sports found the reason was the attitude of the parents who are coaching the developing players. When the coaches have the kids' welfare as the driving force for their volunteering, it becomes a positive experience for those players. When the parents/coaches put their egos in the way and make the experience about themselves, problems arise.

It's like life. Life isn't about the moment at the end or beginning, it's about every step, every moment, doing your best, and appreciating every moment, good and bad. Also, we learn much more from the unpleasant "bad" things than we do from the days we are happy and content. So even losing games has its benefits; losses help people see and thus work on their weaknesses. We cannot always come in first, but we can train and practice with that **Extrinsic Goal** in our hearts and minds. What we need to add are awe and appreciation, which are **Intrinsic Goals** in each moment, and to teach practical techniques that create a sense of wonder about how special is each and every opportunity to compete. I teach these methods to reactivate the spirit of sports to everyone who attends my workshops. It works and it is teachable.

~~~~~~~~

Concept for Transforming the Agony of Winning to the Thrill of Winning:

Learning to appreciate the moment-to-moment engagement in the athletic experience is an important skill to acquire. Letting go of the second-place-is-no-place attitude is rooted in staying present at all times in the purity of athletic competition.

~~~~~~~~

Question for Transforming the Agony of Winning to the Thrill of Winning:

When was the last time you felt a sense of Awe about something that happened in your life? What did it feel like to be in a state of Awe?

~~~~~~~~

Word for Transforming the Agony of Winning to the Thrill of Winning:

Awe

15

Letting Go of the Outcome

The Journey is the Destination

I subscribe to the theory that there are basically three ways in which to view athletic competition. Many participants look at competition as a threat. I think coaches, players, and parents look at the possibility of losing as a challenge to their egos and that somehow a loss will be accompanied by embarrassment. A step up from looking at competition as a threat is to view it as a challenge. The preparation for the sporting event is to meet the challenge the opponent presents.

The prevailing attitude is that other people and/or teams are challenging us. It is us against them. We must rise up and meet this challenge no matter what it takes. The third way to perceive athletic competition is by viewing the games we play through the pure joy that comes from loving the game, win, lose, or draw. I call it falling in love with competition. Another perception that Coach Wooden subscribed to is that you are always competing against yourself. There is not an overwhelming number of athletic participants in this category of competing. You will not find it even on the radar much in this era of sports.

I love this quote from Kay Porter, the womens' cross country coach at the University of Oregon, *"A team can perceive competition in terms of threat, in terms of challenge, or in terms of loving the game. Under threat, a team takes a loss personally. They hold onto it forever. If a team wins under threat, all they do is feel relief. With a challenge, a win makes a team happy. A loss is something to get over. But when a team loves the game, they love the process of the playing itself. They are ecstatic if they win, but if they lose, they just let go of the loss. No team can control what happens all the time. All they can be is responsible for their own reactions."*

I can tell you with confidence that the most prevalent feeling I observe from parents, coaches, and players after winning is relief. After a loss it is an over-the-top feeling of disappointment. I believe most participants view the competition as a threat.

When we make the outcome the most important thing, we lose the "who" and the "why" of athletics because it is in the journey in which teaching opportunities reside. We have turned our backs on the importance of the connection between athletics and education. This system lends itself as a breeding ground for the **Pressure to Succeed** and to getting to that outcome – winning – without paying attention to the integrity of the process. No one, parents, coaches, players, fans, administrators, no one seems immune to the arms race of getting to the end so we can see the result. The **Pressure to Succeed,** which is covered in the Agony of Winning **Strategy Five,** is so unforgiving it lends itself to cheating, coaches being fired if they do win immediately, players enjoying themselves less, and even adopting dangerous personal activities to relieve that pressure.

In the first chapter, I wrote about a high-level college tennis player who resorted to bulimia to relieve the pressure of outcome-based athletics. Lauren was immune to the good feeling of winning because she knew the only thing that mattered at the minute one match ended was what the outcome of her next match would be. I worked with a top gymnast at a major university who had spent his life under the spotlight of, "did you 'hit it'" or in other words, "what was the score on your last routine?" His muted response to getting a high score, which he did often, was matched in the opposite way, in the negative self-criticism when his score was lower than expected — when he did not "hit it."

He and I set out on a five-week course about compassion-based athletics. I taught him that competing was not only about the outcome of his gymnastic meets. I taught him the tenets of Agony **of Winning Strategy Two: Competing with Purpose and Passion.** This young man had so many positives in his experience of preparing for those gymnastic meets, but he had lost or never had an attachment to the absolute brilliance of his journey, the process of training. He had never appreciated his own commitment and hard work. He had never felt satisfaction over the fact that each day he did his best, competing against his best self and others in the gym with effort and integrity. By limiting himself to the score of his routine during the gymnastic meet he lost the entire value of process-based athletics. And that is the Agony of Winning **Strategy Seven: Process-Based Athletics, Letting Go of the Outcome**.

This young man had so much courage. I received from him this e-mail he sent to his teammates. It was his first step establishing a spiritual relationship of inclusion with them, to help them understand, and to include his teammates in the solution.

> *"By now I'm sure almost everybody has seen how I put tape over my forearms each day at practice. The tape is definitely not there to help sore forearm muscles. What lies underneath the pieces of tape are numerous scars that have been put there by me. Cutting has been an almost daily part of my life since sophomore year of high school. Before this year, most of the scars I had were much easier to hide, but as most habits go on, the longer I cut myself the deeper it got and the more places on my body it spread. I simply had not learned the correct way to relieve negative feelings."*

This young man then embarked on a fast track program with me that featured three **Strategies.** Agony of Winning **Strategy Seven: Process-Based Athletics, Letting Go of the Outcome** helped him perceive the absolute joy of training in the gym and that his meet scores were just that, scores. They were not a measurement of his personal worth and value. Then we added in a dose of the Agony of Winning **Strategy Two: Competing with Purpose and Passion.** Here we got him in touch with the joy he felt when he first started competing. We redirected his focus, cut down on his mental distractions, and he began to practice with **Purpose.** Finally I had him begin to get in touch with what was really important in his life. Gymnastics was a big one, but there were many others. I was able to show him that he had a rock solid set of values. All he needed to do was be more cognizant of them. We did this by implementing the guiding principles in the Agony of Winning **Strategy Six: Establishing a System of Core Values.** Read on because you will be amazed at the progress this young man made.

"With the support and encouragement of a couple of the womens' team members, I finally reached out to a professional for guidance. Over the past five weeks of meetings, I have learned new tools to handle negative emotions and turn them to positive feelings. With the new tools in hand, these past few weeks have been the best I can remember in several years. Not only have I not acted out in any way whatsoever in almost a month, but I have gone from thinking about hurting myself or putting myself in harm's way 24 hours a day, seven days a week, to almost not thinking about it at all. I can't begin to explain how monumental this step is for me. I feel that as this habit becomes more under control and a fact of the past, my performance in the gym and the arena will only move upwards.

"I plan to walk into the gym on Friday with my head held high and no tape on my arms. If you look where

the tape was, you will see the marks. They are there and I cannot simply erase them. I do not need to feel ashamed or closed in about the situation anymore around the people who care about me and whom I care about so much. The people here are some of the best I have ever met and I would not trade this for anything. As once said by Maria Robinson, 'Nobody can go back and start a new beginning, but anyone can start today and make a new ending.'"

This young man incorporated the Agony of Winning **Strategies** and is moving in the right direction in his life. These **7 Strategies** are very teachable and effective when put into action.

In the all-out effort to secure a favorable outcome, coaches, good men and women, have forgotten to maintain the tenets of the Agony of Winning **Strategy Six: Establishing a System of Core Values.**

Without a system in place to combat the pressure cooker of athletics, coaches fall victim to attaching themselves to the outcome.

Dave Bliss, who is the former mens' basketball coach at Baylor, puts it this way, *"Cheating is a performance-enhancing drug. People don't need to cheat; I didn't need to cheat. Why do it? Our obsession to try and better our situations."* This is what I mean by the arms race in athletics, the mentality that if we do not do it someone else will. He continues, *"You try to create different advantages – not cheating, but pretty soon the gray goes to the illegal area. And that's what happened to me."* These actions are taken to ensure a better outcome.

It is this pressure, combined with a lack of ethics, that leads athletes to take performance-enhancing drugs. Janet Evans, an Olympic gold medalist in swimming, actually bragged about the fact that a greasy swimsuit had a lot to do with her win.

"It is Not Whether You Win or Lose but How You Play the Game." I think you could get hurt today if you were sitting in the bleachers of any sporting event and uttered these words with sincerity. It is not one of the hot quotes that coaches are using, either. Forget the media; I have not seen these particular words of wisdom hop off the page at me in a while. Actually, that quote isn't the real quote on the topic of giving it your all and not letting the outcome become the most important factor of the athletic experience.

Check out the real quote from Grantland Rice Alumnus Football:

> **"You'll find the road is long and rough,**
> **with soft spots far apart,**
> **Where only those can make the grade**
> **who have the Uphill Heart.**
> **And when they stop you with a thud**
> **or halt you with a crack,**
> **Let Courage call the signals**
> **as you keep on coming back.**
>
> **"Keep coming back, and though the world**
> **may romp across your spine,**
> **Let every game's end find you still**
> **upon the battling line;**
> **For when the One Great Scorer comes**
> **to mark against your name,**
> **He writes — not that you won or lost —**
> **but how you played the Game."**

OK, so a little poetic justice was employed in the interpretation of what old Grantland was trying to say here. It looks to me like he was talking about something bigger than an athletic contest. In my mind, he is discussing the game of life; heaven and hell seem to be the outcomes he is reflecting on. However, since sports are merely a microcosm of life it is adaptable to athletics as well. Grantland hit it right on the noggin that sports ought to be about THE JOURNEY, THE PROCESS. He urges us to keep coming back, even if the world may romp across your spine, or your opponent is kicking your butt. When the game is over, whether it be an athletic game or the game of life, let it find you not diminished but standing tall upon the battling line. The purpose of athletics is the process. **The Agony of Winning Strategy Seven: Process-Based Athletics, Letting Go of the Outcome** teaches that.

Coach Mike Ricci, the basketball coach at Haddon Heights High School in New Jersey, is rooted in coaching and concerned about what his players are learning on the way to the victories. I got this e-mail from him:

> *"I have been coaching high school sports since I was 21, that's 18 years. Wow, talking about that and seeing that in writing are 2 different things! Anyway, I was always good at the Xs and Os, and I realized as I matured as a coach that although winning was important, winning the right way was even more important.* **Teaching kids how to be leaders, sportsmanship, accountability, and especially personal responsibility is really where I do my most coaching.**
>
> *I have coached many kids over the years, and some of the most challenging kids I ever had to coach (and they had*

the most talent too by the way) are the ones I have the best relationships with today. There was nothing more satisfying than this past season as we went through our season, made the playoffs and after one of my games, a player who I coached in Paulsboro, Soloman Sheard, walked up to me after the game and gave me a big hug and said he heard I was coaching at Haddon Heights and he wanted to stop by. We talked for 20 minutes after that game about his life, his family. He started talking about memories from when I coached him and then some of the lessons he learned. It was music to my ears. It made me so happy and of course proud. The next day, he showed up a practice to help our young kids. It was a great moment."

It is obvious that Coach Ricci has his **Core Values** in the right place.

To me the Grantland Rice quote means that whether you win or lose, it is always about the next step. Just like the Kean University softball team. The integrity of your next move is the important thing. If in the process of doing your best, of not backing down, of challenging yourself in each and every moment to be, to do, and to act in a way characterized by 100% effort, winning is much more likely. I should be clear that winning feels better than losing, and it is a lot more fun. However, winning is not the most important thing unless we reduce the whole athletic experience to this one limited measurement of success. The world of athletics has lost its way and simply forgotten the message in the Agony of Winning **Strategy Two: Competing with Purpose and Passion.**

The outcome means a lot of things; I view an outcome as something that follows as a result or consequence. I think a very important aspect of that definition would be the word "consequence." The world of sports has started a domino effect of negative consequences because of the singular emphasis on the end result of winning. In fact, as I have pointed out in other chapters, winning is no longer good enough. Actually, I have seen a change over the last 20 years that dictates that the only acceptable outcome for participation in athletics is being No. 1.

To be fair, occasional news reports include information on what sports would be like if we competed with compassion. If we understood that the real joy is in the journey or process of going after that important end result. It is important to have an end goal, an end result to add validity to the journey. The end result is important, just not the most important thing. However, when I read the Haddonfield, New Jersey, Middle School philosophy statement for athletics it gave me hope that protecting the spirit and integrity of sport is a priority in some venues. The following philosophy was adopted by the Haddonfield school board. The school mandated that the athletic director hire coaches who would adhere to the philosophy and assess the current coaches in the same manner. The philosophy statement:

"The activity and athletic programs of Haddonfield Middle School help students to develop a positive self-image, foster a sense of belonging, and increase student interest and participation in extra-curricular activities that will extend into high school, college, and community. In addition, the programs are designed to foster the development of life skills, positive values, leadership, service, and healthy habits so that personal

growth and development and improvement, personal
best and cooperation and team spirit, rather than focus
on the high levels of performance/competition."

The school also recognizes that passion may be diminished when the athletes are exposed to a win-at-all-costs approach to athletics. They are RIGHT.

The world of sports emphasizes the wrong things. The end results we want our athletes to derive from their sports participation are those character traits the Haddonfield Board of Education deemed important in its philosophy statement. These end results have a longer-lasting effect on the athlete, the school, the families of the athletes, and the community as a whole. The pursuit of excellence through striving for an end result that includes these elements makes athletics more relevant and noble as an education tool. Merely having end results that solely emphasize winning, scholarships, awards, etc., has little long-lasting benefit.

In the year I am penning this book, Joe Paterno, the famous head football coach of the Penn State team, is 82 years old. It is amazing that he is still coaching. He began his coaching career in an entirely different era. Actually, several eras ago. The spirit of sport and the end results that I laid out in the previous paragraph were prevalent when he started coaching. In a news story in the *Philadelphia Inquirer,* Frank Fitzpatrick writes that in the '70s and '80s Paterno *"...talked a lot back then about something called the 'Grand Experiment.' In many ways Coach Paterno was viewed as someone who ran a very 'clean' program without recruiting violations or sanctions from the NCAA. Fitzpatrick described the philosophy as '...one that emphasized academics and integrity as much as bowl games.' Funny, but you don't hear Joe Pa mention the ex-*

periment much these days. Some of that reluctance stems from the fact that the old coach is afraid that he sounds too sanctimonious ...But it is also present because Paterno is smart enough to realize the battle is lost." That is a sad statement of affairs.

However, I believe a model that incorporates values, spirit, and integrity in the modern era is not only needed but very possible. This book is a guideline for incorporating that model. It really comes down to making a decision that sports is more than just about winning and losing. If we were to simply take the world of sports as it is and add back in the ingredients that enhance sports' possibilities as an educational tool, we would increase the likelihood that athletic competition could reach its lofty potential. Athletics can be an empty experience when losing is treated like a bad disease and winning become a mundane experience and feels like the Agony of Winning.

The notion that preparing and training for an athletic contest is an arduous process at best and its only value is its outcome is perpetuated in the professional ranks. And yes, the attitude filters down to the youngest of athletes. That philosophy professes that training and practice bring with it one outcome, that it prepares you to play in a game. If that game does not result in a win, then the training has no value.

I am challenging high school and college administrators to put in place an evaluation system for coaches that measures more than wins and losses because we have turned our back on the principles taught in the Agony of Winning **Strategy Seven: Process-Based Athletics, Letting Go of the Outcome**. In addition, the administrators could take a look at the tenets and principles inside two other strategies — the Agony of Winning **Strategy Two: Competing with Purpose**

and Passion and the Agony of Winning Strategy **Six: Establishing a System of Core Values** – and integrate them into their evaluations of their coaches. If they did so they would be operating a compassion-based athletic program and have that system in place without sacrificing winning. It requires, however, a commitment to the Agony of Winning Triangle, which is the first **Strategy,** that commitment of time to ensure we are not just teaching the "what" of athletics but the "who" and the "why."

Turning away from the philosophy that athletics plays a role in the educational mission of the university has a devastating effect on everyone. It is folly to divorce the mission of what athletics could represent from a teaching perspective from the educational mission as a whole. The adoption of that particular point of view has left us without a process by which to evaluate the effectiveness of coaches and players that goes beyond winning and losing. For instance, if a coach is providing an opportunity for their players to grow as people but does not win enough games they may not get fired in a system that competes with compassion. Since winning is important as an outcome of playing games, of course it is a factor in the evaluation of the coach. However, within the confines of the current system, too often it seems to matter little who the coaches and players are and why they are competing as long as they do what they do well. That has to be altered because it is making its way down to high school athletics, as I pointed out in another chapter.

However, the good news is that many coaches, like those mentioned in these pages, are getting it about process-based athletics. One of those coaches, Al Golden, wrote the foreword to this book. This amazing man with much success as the head football coach at Temple University wrote the following in the foreword, and it is worth repeating here:

> *"As the head football coach of a program that transformed from one win in 2006 to nine wins and our first bowl game in thirty years in 2009, I can share with you that it was our unwavering commitment to executing a process both on and off the field where core values and life-skill development served as the foundation that resulted in this cultural transformation. The 2009 Temple Football Owls are a testimony to how Kevin Touhey's philosophy and approach to coaching is successful even in the most challenging of circumstances."*

The time I spent with Coach talking about process-based athletics solidified my belief that it is possible to pay attention to the educational integrity of using athletics as a major avenue to teach life lessons and win big.

Concept for Transforming the Agony of Winning to the Thrill of Winning:

It is the journey and process of competing that is most important. It is all about doing your best in each moment, in other words, how you play the game. It is also in the process where you can learn the most about yourself.

Question for Transforming the Agony of Winning to the Thrill of Winning:

What would it take for you let go of the outcome and concentrate on your moment-to-moment relationship with athletic competition?

Word for Transforming the Agony of Winning to the Thrill of Winning:

Present

16

Temple University Football

The Epitome of Values-Based Winning

I asked my Coaching Principles class at Drexel University why coaches do not understand that a team can be wildly successful in terms of wins and losses and run a values-based program. They are hard-pressed to come up with an answer. The timing of this book coincides perfectly with the story of a college football program that has done precisely that. This program has become a winning program because the head coach was committed to establishing a set of core values within each player. The result of working on the "I" in team has been an entire program based on a "we" mentality. There is a very large measure of accountability and consequences built right into the culture of the Temple University Football program.

There will be a moment when Coach Al Golden will hoist the National Championship Trophy above his head. He will have accomplished the feat while running a program based on the Agony of Winning **Strategy Six: Establishing a System of Core Values** and the Agony of Winning **Strategy Seven: Process-Based Athletics, Letting Go of the Outcome**. In my discussions I asked Coach Golden the following question: *"How is it that you could take over a program in the sad shape that this one was in and not feel the pressure?"* He responded by saying, *"Kevin, I have long applied the philosophy that you have laid out in this book without ever having met you before. I do not look beyond the everyday process and journey in building the program. I know the results will come if I just focus on the journey. I know if I take every step with integrity there is no pressure because I am only focused on the moment."*

Great answer, don't you think?

I followed that question with this one, *"Coach, why core values, why take the time it requires to continually teach and hold your team accountable to an ethical approach to training?"* He answered by saying, *"Number one, it is the right thing to do if we are going to teach players to be accountable and responsible to a higher level of integrity. In addition, ultimately it makes coaching easier when the culture shifts as a result of the players buying in and perpetuating the idea that doing the right thing in the process brings the desired outcomes."*

Coach Al Golden accepted the challenge of fixing a broken-down college football program and has produced one of the greatest turnarounds perhaps in all of Division I-A football history. His vehicle was establishing a football program built around a set of core values. When he arrived on campus, he discovered a worn-out program suffering from neglect. The program was left rudderless by the coaches that had preceded him. Those coaches did not want to spend the time developing young men. Instead of dwelling on the negatives about Temple's situation, Golden embraced the positives. He brought with him a goal to emphasize the life lessons required for teams to win, and more importantly, to win with dignity and honor.

I found a blog written by one of the seniors on the 2009 Temple football team. This is an incredible endorsement of what Coach Golden established at Temple University. This entry was written by starting tight end Steve Maneri in December 2009. He is a senior who was in Coach Golden's first recruiting class and writes:

> *"There were seniors who were thrown off the team, seniors who quit, and seniors who got suspended for fights, academic miscues, or anything else you can think of. I could tell you that today if one of my seniors stopped showing up, there would be 10 of us lined up at the coaches' doors trying to figure out what happened and what we can do to get him back. But thankfully, that's not an issue anymore, because those boys who ran onto that field in 2006, those boys who got their butts kicked by a combined score of 496-131, those boys who were the laughing stock of college football, those boys became men."*

In talking with him it was easy to ascertain that Coach Golden has at his own **Core;** the **Values** he teaches his team. He knows that discipline, academics, empowering the players to succeed, and community service are all "who" and "why" aspects of athletics that contribute to the players' lives and produce a program that succeeds with excellence, from the inside out.

"I found a lot of young men who had lost hope and we needed to start educating," Golden said. *"You have to start to implement your culture and your core values. As you evolve, you have a lot of people who aren't willing to make those sacrifices. So many of them had to move on."* Sacrifice is a baseline core value that must be established in each player so the whole can succeed.

The Agony of Winning **Strategy Six: Establishing a System of Core Values** has **Personal Sacrifice** as one of its core principles. **Personal Sacrifice** is one of the core values the Temple University football players have tapped into in a big way. More comments from Steve Maneri:

"Sacrifice. Playing football for Temple is not just a team sport or an extra-curricular activity; it's a way of life. Even the weekends in the offseason, when guys are letting loose, there is still a standard to represent. One of my teammates had another person challenge him while he was out socializing last summer. You know what my teammate did? He walked away. And it has nothing to do with fear, because my teammate easily could have had the upper hand in an altercation. He sacrificed his pride for the greater good of the team. The guy who challenged him was a person with nothing to lose, and doing anything other than walk away, would do nothing but hurt the team." This is a prime example of the "I," the individual

player, learning a **Core Value** and putting it into practice in the process and journey of being a Temple University football player for the team.

The object of playing the game is to win. Winning is an **Extrinsic** goal that is very important, but what Coach Golden found at Temple was a well-established culture of losing. He knew that had to change. What I love about his methods is that he knew, *"We had to change that from the inside out. It's an arduous process. You have to be methodical. You can't flinch. You have to implement your core values and be steadfast in your support and defense of those values."*

You see, Coach knew by rewarding the "who" and the 'why" that the "what" would improve. His reward system included recognition of players who excelled not just on the practice field but in the classroom, the weight room, and in the community. He established a perfect combination of intrinsic and extrinsic goals.

Maneri shares this insight:

"When Coach Golden first got to Temple, he started laying the bricks for a foundation, which meant lots and lots of rules. The id is no longer calling the shots. Now when that girl hits one of us up at 10 p.m. on a Tuesday during game week, or when we get invited to the Kappa Sig party on a Thursday, our upcoming game is usually helping us make that decision. Any Joe Schmo can down a few beverages at a party, but it takes men to have a goal and sacrifice whatever needs to be sacrificed in order to achieve that goal."

Maneri is a product of a program that knows the Thrill of Winning because he plays for a coach in a program that understands that athletics is a great opportunity to teach young people how to become better players and better people. It is lazy thinking and selfish for coaches to not incorporate the life lessons inherent in the "who" and the "why" into their programs. We owe it to every athlete who participates to teach them the basics of becoming better people through their involvement. We need to tap into the Lofty Potential of what sports has to teach and stop reducing it to a win-loss record. One of the Core Values Steve Maneri learned was an awareness of the Agony of Winning **Strategy Six: Establishing a System of Core Values** has **Personal Sacrifice,** the Coach Golden version.

More from Maneri's post gives us some insight into being accountable for what you say you will commit to. This entry includes another important value espoused in the pages of this book: integrity.

> *"What does becoming men really mean? Isn't every idiot who grew hair on his chest considered a man in today's society? Sigmund Freud believed that everyone was born with an id. Having an id basically means that you are compelled to do whatever makes you feel good at the time without any regards for situation. As children matured, they began to develop awareness of their surroundings and eventually morals and values. Their decisions reflected these values."*

It is so refreshing to hear a college football player mention morals and values. However, these are not just words; these young men have turned those words into actions. This coach and his team walk the talk. Maneri, also was part of a program that has a system of responsibility and accountability for each individual in relation to the whole. This is a program that has **The Thrill of Winning** at its core as a result of paying attention to who and the why of the journey to winning.

> *"In my four years at Temple, I'm proud to say that I've been part of one of the biggest four-year turnarounds in college football history. However, while the outside world only sees the finished product, I'm here to tell you that there was a lot more to the story than just Xs and Os. Coach Golden took a group of 18-year-old kids, and relentlessly molded us in to the men that we are today."*

If coaches will take the time to broaden the scope of their program they will be under less stress and they will not have to sacrifice winning; however, they will more fully enjoy the true rewards of coaching, which are teaching themselves and their players important life lessons. Coach Golden insisted his players understand that they needed to be of service to the whole program. He made sure that the program did not get bogged down with distractions brought on by selfish players. An insight into his philosophy is revealed in this statement by Golden:

> *"We wanted them to see the big picture on how their decisions impacted the community and university. Ultimately, it would lead to winning behavior. Winning behavior begets winning. We wanted to find some things we could be successful at because it certainly was going to be quite some time before we could be successful on the field."*

Coach Golden has married, in perfect fashion, the **Intrin-**

sic and **Extrinsic values** that make a program excellent. I am proud of my own 35-year affiliation with the Temple University football program. In fact, I have never been more proud.

~~~~~~~~

Concept for Transforming the Agony of Winning to the Thrill of Winning:

*It is imperative that all of us in athletics begin to incorporate a set of **Core Values** under which to operate. It is also important that we require a system of accountability that ensures we adhere to those stated **Values** while competing.*

~~~~~~~~

Question for Transforming the Agony of Winning to the Thrill of Winning:

*What **Core Values** would you like to see incorporated into athletic competition? What would be the desired outcome of establishing those **Values**?*

~~~~~~~~

Word for Transforming the Agony of Winning to the Thrill of Winning:

Sacrifice

Epilogue

The Thrill of Winning is Back

Many adults seem to have forgotten what it means to be a kid. We played sports a lot of the time just to be social; however, we did not have an adult teaching us to crush the opponent. In fact, we played so many games that kids who were our teammates for one game became an opponent the next game. I can even remember changing teams in the middle of the game when the teams became imbalanced and the game was not competitive enough. You see, the exhilaration of playing was our attachment to the spirit of the competition itself. It was not fun if the game was not evenly matched. We wanted to have a competitive game; we did not need an adult laying out the rules for us.

We did not lack the desire to be competitive, but we were exhibiting the principles of The Agony of Winning **Strategy Three: Maintaining a Balance of Intrinsic and Extrinsic Goals** without even knowing it. We were so attached to the feeling of exhilaration, that soaring feeling of competing as if each game we played was Game 7 of the World Series. Make no mistake, we all had the **Extrinsic Goal** of making tackles, hitting homers, and making the game winning hoop, as well as beating our friends. However, the **Intrinsic Goals** were present also. In another chapter I mentioned my work with the Cherokee Football Team, which I helped set **Intrinsic** goals. In years past we also had **Intrinsic** goals playing in the free range environment. We were deriving the same things from competition as the Cherokee Football team: *Enjoyment and Relaxation, Friendship and Relationships, Playing with a Sense of Purpose and Passion, Appreciate One Another, A Basic Love of Competition, Have a Lot of Fun, and Feel Part of Something.* Back then it happened as a result of the free play experience, but in today's world the Agony of Winning principles of **Maintaining a Balance of Intrinsic and Extrinsic Goals** must be taught. They will not happen naturally because athletes have very little free time.

We required no interference from adults, but we were competitive, to say the least. **Strategy Two: Competing with Purpose and Passion** was evident in our competitive spirit. We played with passion and because we had a balance **of Goals, Intrinsic** and **Extrinsic,** our **Passion** was evident on each and every play. No one needed to motivate us, we did that ourselves and were pushed by our teammates, with no adults allowed. We knew our **Purpose,** and we attacked it with enthusiasm and vigor.

Our fights with each other over rules, safe/out calls, in-bounds, and whether the teams were fair were handled by us. By the way, those fights were always left on the field. When the game was over we went home friends. Although today we must teach these principles on purpose and with intention, back then we had our own **Strategy Four:** the Agony of Winning **Code of Ethics: Setting a Tone for Integrity, Respect, and Civility.** We learned a code of conduct. We policed it ourselves and held each other accountable to it. We knew it was not going to be fun if we did not, and that was one of our main **Purposes for Playing,** to have fun.

Strategy One: the Agony of Winning **Triangle: The "Who," "What," and "Why" of Athletics** was always evident. We played hard, and the technical skills, or the "what" of our playing, was important. We all wanted to get better, not to win a trophy but to get chosen a little quicker when teams were picked the next time we played. We wanted to improve our "what" so that we might get to take the last shot of the game to win it, or be the player who was passed to for the winning score. We were not thinking about earning a college scholarship in the years to come. "Who" we were was also important. Tempers would flare, arguments would occur, occasionally a player would pout if he was not being included enough in the plays being run, or was batting too low in the order. However, we all knew our "why," which was our underlying motivation or passion for playing. That "why" would be the key, just like it is today, for setting the tone of our playing experience. We were aware of our "why" on a very deep level without talking about it. We understood, better than most adults, that what we were doing was just a game and was supposed to be enjoyed.

In the foreword of the book, Coach Al Golden points out that the essence of competition itself is in reality fun. He then quotes tennis coach and renowned mental coach W. Timothy Gallwey. In his book *The Inner Game of Tennis*, he points out that the three cornerstones of the Inner Game are performance, learning, <u>AND enjoyment.</u> The important thing is that it was fun just playing and competing and we knew that on the deepest level of our souls.

If you struck out, missed a wide open jumper, or fumbled on the goal line it was forgotten quickly. We adhered to the principles in the Agony of Winning **Strategy Seven: Process-Based Athletics, Letting Go of the Outcome**. We knew that the most important thing was the next play, the next game, or the maybe we even had to wait until the next time we played. There was no adult reminding us what our miscue cost us. There were no costs, no awards or first place trophies, no proper seeding in the third-grade playoff tournament. At the worst, our game-costing mistake would bring some good-natured chiding by the rest of the kids as we walked home after the game.

In almost all cases, when there was a dispute it was dealt with by the time we were ready to walk home or in between games when new teams were being picked. If you did "blow" the game by dropping the game-winning pass, struck out with the bases loaded and the tying run at third, or missed that game-tying jumper on your last possession, there was not a huge price for your self-esteem to pay. Maybe a small nick in your pride but no burden of making sure the coach, or Mommy and Daddy's pride didn't have a huge dent in it for the whole sporting world to see. The over regulation of youth sports by adults is putting a huge measure of expectation on players today.

These young athletes do not have much free play time without parental or coaching interference. The young athletes of today do not get enough time to experience the exhilaration of free play unencumbered by rules or direction from adults. It is almost impossible for the developing athlete to learn about compassion for athletic competition because an adult is always grooming them from a younger-than-ever age to beat an opponent.

When adults have four- and five-year-olds signing up for soccer and football in structured programs where the rules are laid out for them, we leave little room for them to experiment with imaginary teams and rules. These structured environments preclude the valuable lessons learned by young athletes setting up their own teams with imaginary season schedules and league standings. It eliminates make-believe championships, the tracking of their own touchdown totals and fielding percentages, tackles, and batting averages. It eliminates the exhilaration of being in the make-believe uniform of their favorite sport teams and heroes. They are already being fitted for their own uniforms assigned to them by adults. The principles taught in the the Agony of Winning **Strategy Five: Overcoming the Pressure to Succeed** *are necessary in today's high-stress athletic environment. It needs to start with the youngest of athletes. However, as you can see by reading some of the stories in the chapters of this book, the Agony of Winning is being felt by competitors of all ages.*

I know those days are gone forever. I do not expect to walk out of my back yard onto the Allen School playground and see a caged window or a chalk outline of the strike zone used in the stick ball games of my youth. I do not expect to see the adjacent blacktop basketball court bustling with players engaged in a fierce game of pick-up. In those games played up to 10 points, a team must win by 2 points, if your team won you stayed on and played in the next game. If your team lost you got off the court and waited for your next chance to play in another game, that is, if you even got another chance to get on the court again.

Those stick ball "stadiums" and endless pick-up games on the outdoor basketball "arenas" are empty today. I am not suggesting we can go back to the way it used to be, NOT GOING TO HAPPEN. However, this book has provided the reader with a road map on how to move into the future with a way to make athletics joyful again. Ultimately, I am not trying to turn back the hands of time to that sentimental era. Rather the message of the book merely adds the missing ingredient – enjoyment – back into the mix. The Agony of Winning **Strategies** teaches the athlete how to develop better self-esteem, to become a good teammate, and to feel the basic human need of being included and appreciated. It teaches the athlete how to cheer for the success of others as well as himself or herself, to demonstrate leadership capabilities, and to be cooperative and of service to others. The Strategies teach the participants in athlete competition to understand that by challenging themselves to be motivated, enjoy, and do their absolute best the entire time they are practicing and playing, they will learn the most about themselves in those moments.

We need to teach to coaches, athletes, and parents that all the real gold in athletics is in paying attention to the process. It is not going to happen naturally because there is no venue for that any longer for the youngest of athletes. We have to take the time and create the venue. The old venue is closed. What needs to happen in the world of sports today is also alluded to in the foreword by Coach Golden; he writes, *"The essence of training, preparation, skill development and pushing yourself should be enjoyment and personal fulfillment. It does not have to be drudgery. Kevin steadfastly believes that this feeling needs to be restored into organized sport and needs to commence at the youth level."*

LaVergne, TN USA
22 October 2010
201991LV00002B/122/P

Modern L... ion of America

Research and Scholarship in Composition

Lil Brannon, Anne Ruggles Gere, Dixie... Comp...,
C. H. Knoblauch, Geneva Smitherman-Donaldson... Young,
Series Editors

1. Anne Herrington and Charles Moran, eds. *Writing, Teaching, and Learning in the Disciplines.* 1992.
2. Cynthia L. Selfe and Susan Hilligoss, eds. *Literacy and Computers: The Complications of Teaching and Learning with Technology.* 1993.
3. John Clifford and John Schilb, eds. *Writing Theory and Critical Theory.* 1994.

The Modern Language Association of America
New York   1994

e following publishers have generously granted permission for the use of
tended quotations from copyrighted works: "Democracy," from *The Wild
ag* (Houghton Mifflin). © 1943, 1971 by E. B. White. Originally in the *New
orker*. Guidelines accompanying E. B. White's essay "Democracy" in *The
lorton Reader*, edited by Arthur M. Eastman. Seventh edition (Norton,
988). "Tribute," from the *New Yorker*. © 1943, 1971 by The New Yorker
Magazine, Inc.

Library of Congress Cataloging-in-Publication Data

Writing theory and critical theory / edited by John Clifford and John
    Schilb.
        p.   cm. — (Research and scholarship in composition ; 3)
    Includes bibliographical references and index.
    ISBN 0-87352-575-2 ISBN 0-87352-576-0 (pbk.)
        1. English language—Rhetoric—Study and teaching—Theory. etc.
    2. Literature—History and criticism—Theory, etc.   3. Criticism.
    I. Clifford, John.   II. Schilb, John, 1952–   III. Series.
    PE1404.W744   1994
    808′.042—dc20   93-50595

Published by The Modern Language Association of America
10 Astor Place, New York, New York 10003-6981

Set in New Aster

Printed on recycled paper

Contents

Responses to Part IV

Preface to the Series

The Research and Scholarship in Composition series, developed with the support of the Modern Language Association's Publications Committee, responds to the recent growth of interest in composition and to the remarkable number of publications now devoted to it. We intend the series to provide a carefully coordinated overview of the varied theoretical schools, educational philosophies, institutional groupings, classroom situations, and pedagogical practices that collectively constitute the major areas of inquiry in the field of composition studies.

Each volume combines theory, research, and practice in order to clarify theoretical issues, synthesize research and scholarship, and improve the quality of writing instruction. Further, each volume reviews the most significant issues in a particular area of composition research and instruction; reflects on ways research and teaching inform each other; views composition studies in the larger context of literary, literacy, and cultural studies; and draws conclusions from various scholarly perspectives about what has been done and what yet needs to be done in the field.

We hope this series will serve a wide audience of teachers, scholars, and students who are interested in the teaching of writing, research in composition, and the connections among composition, literature, and other areas of study. These volumes should act as a lively orientation to the field for students and nonspecialists and provide experienced teachers and scholars with useful overviews of research on important questions, with insightful reflections about teaching, and with thoughtful analyses about future developments in composition studies. Each book is a spirited conversation in which you are cordially invited to join.

Series Editors

Introduction

This volume of original essays is the third in a series designed to meet the need for "a carefully coordinated overview" of the "major areas of inquiry in the field of composition studies." When we started to plan *Writing Theory and Critical Theory*, we indeed felt able to define "the most significant issues" that connected the words of our title. When we made an open call for submissions, however, we encountered a formidable range of perspectives on our topic. Even when we solicited essays from scholars familiar to us, we often failed to anticipate what they would eventually write. Of course, this collection does not simply parade idiosyncratic views; rather, it features several recurring themes that our own dispositions have helped shape. Nevertheless, the book can lead authors, editors, and, yes, readers down unexpected paths. As with research on other topics in this series, the body of work linking writing theory and critical theory continues to grow in many ways. In introducing the following essays, we inevitably propose a certain framework; at the same time, we acknowledge that it is inevitably provisional.

Even the book's title reflects decisions we have made. The term *writing theory* can denote trends related to writing, rhetoric, and composition. To be frank, we feel less secure with our other key term, *critical theory*. We mean it to indicate various strands of contemporary thinking that have influenced literary studies, including deconstruction, hermeneutics, postmodernism, feminism, neo-Marxism, neopragmatism, psychoanalysis, reader response, and cultural studies. The series editors originally proposed the term *literary theory*, but we ultimately decided against this term, for two reasons. First, the schools of thought we have cited transcend literary studies; they infuse other fields like philosophy, history, and the social sciences. Second, literary scholars themselves have drawn on these schools to question the very idea of "literature" as a unique (and uniquely valuable) mode of discourse.

We follow many advocates of these approaches when we turn to *critical theory* as an alternative rubric. It has the virtue of signaling a

1

preoccupation of all these schools: critique of current discursive practices and social structures. As a term, *critical theory* is somewhat prob-
lematic because of its original association with the Frankfurt school,
a circle of German cultural critics who fled to the United States during
World War II. Members of this group—including Theodor Adorno,
Max Horkheimer, and Herbert Marcuse—did hold some ideas peculiar
to them. In one form or another, though, several of their concerns have
reemerged for the contemporary theories that we have in mind. Even
if these theories do not use the Frankfurt school's vocabulary or adopt
its orientation, they pursue some of its characteristic themes: the illu-
sions of Enlightenment rationality, the nature of political authority,
the construction of human subjects, the role of language in mental
representations, the power of mass culture, the need for self-reflection,
and the need to adapt previous social theories to modern (or postmod-
ern) circumstances.

We became acutely conscious of recent developments linking writing
theory and critical theory when we looked back at an earlier essay that
we wrote on this topic. Entitled "Composition Theory and Literary
Theory," it appeared in the 1985 MLA volume *Perspectives on Research
and Scholarship in Composition*. In the essay, we attended most to
reader-response theorists, because they joined many composition
scholars in depicting students as active shapers of meaning. We noted
that a few specialists in composition were turning to deconstruction
or to other forms of poststructuralism, and we pointed out that various
scholars were proposing *rhetoric* as a rubric for unifying English studies. We concluded by highlighting two opposing curricular visions:
Terry Eagleton's notion of rhetoric as the study of mass culture and E.
D. Hirsch's "cultural literacy," which we equated with support of the
canon. (Subsequently Hirsch dissociated himself from the great-books
curriculum while continuing to advocate the teaching of mainstream
knowledge.)

A good deal has changed since we wrote that essay. At that time, we
focused on composition and literature as unified entities that needed
to overcome the differences *between* them. Recent history indicates
growing differences *within* these fields. Scholars now argue regularly
about what the mission, methodology, and content of each field should
be. For example, as David Shumway notes in this volume, empirical
research has become a subject of intense debate in composition after
dominating the field for almost two decades. Both composition and
literature have spawned theory and antitheory camps; in her essay,
Beth Daniell analyzes composition's version of this trend. Since 1985
certain visions of a unified English curriculum have also emerged or

grown stronger. Nowadays many English faculty members wish not simply to amalgamate composition and literature but, rather, to elaborate a third term that would displace or subsume them. As Susan Miller and Kathleen McCormick indicate in their essays, one new candidate is *cultural studies*. An increasing number of scholars in literature as well as composition have turned to *rhetoric* as a possible disciplinary framework; see, for example, the proceedings of the 1987 MLA conference on doctoral programs in English (Lunsford, Moglen, and Slevin).

There is as yet no consensus on how to define these two terms. Scholars in literature and composition still need to decide which methodologies and topics constitute the purview of cultural studies (Schilb, "Cultural Studies"), and a tension still exists between classical and deconstructive understandings of rhetoric. The classical view associates rhetoric with persuasion, while the deconstructive view focuses on the destabilizing interplay of tropes. Many composition specialists insist on the continued viability of the classical tradition (see Murphy; Connors, Ede, and Lunsford). The contributors to this volume do not oppose classical rhetoric; some, including Suzanne Clark and Susan Wells, explicitly value elements of it. But, in keeping with the book's title, most primarily investigate the resources that deconstruction and other forms of critical theory can bring to the study of discourse. Rather than see deconstruction as an end in itself, these authors, like many current theorists, enlist its strategies for the larger purpose of cultural critique. When they focus on linguistic instability, they ultimately relate it to particular social actions at particular moments in history. Several of the contributors—for example, Susan Miller, Kathleen McCormick, Kurt Spellmeyer, James Slevin, Linda Brodkey, and Victor Villanueva—attempt to fuse rhetoric with cultural studies and to give clear new dimensions to each.

The school of thought that we emphasized years ago, reader-response theory, still thrives in composition and literary studies. Yet, under the surging influence of feminism, neo-Marxism, minority perspectives, postcolonial thought, and the work of Michel Foucault, reader-response theorists in both fields have increasingly turned to ideological critique. They see readers and writers not as free, individual agents but, rather, as the products of discourses that frequently serve the state. Reader-response theory continues to examine individual reading and writing performances. Now, however, it often analyzes them as modes of subjection or resistance to dominant institutions. This approach, too, appears throughout the essays that follow. Most notably, Slevin analyzes the ways in which composition students are themselves constructed as *Norton* readers.

In effect, several of the essays in this volume critique a movement that we did not forecast in 1985: social constructionism. It was introduced to composition by theorists like Kenneth Bruffee, Patricia Bizzell, and Elaine Maimon. They in turn drew on neopragmatists like Richard Rorty and Stanley Fish, who emphasized the incorrigibly social foundations of human thought. This movement usefully disputed composition's previous emphasis on the isolated writer and acontextual skills. As a result, a flood of scholarship emerged that identified ways in which writing demands vary with context, a prime example being the differing standards of the academic disciplines. Many composition specialists, however, now question aspects of this trend. Clark, in her essay here, worries that it may once again purge emotion from academic reason. As Spellmeyer indicates, many suspect that conventions do not regulate discourse as much as social constructionism has claimed they do. He also makes the increasingly familiar charge that social constructionism emphasizes conformity. Several contributors, whether or not they fault this movement explicitly, call for a more radical criticism of existing institutions. They believe that composition should not just invoke "the social" and proceed to affirm particular discourses; for them, the various components of "the social" must be anatomized, evaluated, and quite possibly transformed.

Such analysis must include English departments themselves. As institutions, they shape whatever relations can be posited between writing theory and critical theory in the first place. When we discussed the possible relations between the two in 1985, we chose not to dwell on the historically low status of composition in the English curriculum. In part, we wanted to emphasize developments in theory; in part, we hoped that the situation of writing instructors would improve. Since then, composition has indeed gained respect as a field, as the very existence of this MLA series attests. The number of graduate programs in composition and rhetoric has increased and so has the number of tenure-track positions. Nevertheless, many English departments have yet to give composition a status equal to that of literature. They continue to regard the interpretation of poetry, fiction, and drama as inherently more valuable and to relegate composition to overworked, underpaid graduate students or part-timers. They identify composition with teaching, and teaching with mere service to the rest of the college or university. Various contributors allude explicitly to these circumstances, including Susan Miller, Kurt Spellmeyer, Sharon Crowley, and Ross Winterowd. We suspect, however, that all the contributors want English departments to grant composition genuine parity. After all, relations between writing theory and critical theory are not just theoretical; they emerge from, and impinge on, people's working lives. While the specific curricular visions proposed here vary, they reflect a common imperative: to challenge systems that disenfranchise people by narrowing the available discourse. English departments, because they continue to marginalize the field most responsible for identifying possibilities of discourse, cannot be exempt from this critique.

We have organized the volume into four sections, although we are aware that their concerns overlap. The essays in "Refiguring Traditions" propose ways of using critical theory to historicize and assess orthodoxies of writing instruction. First, Susan Miller submits that British cultural studies and related schools of thought can help composition rethink its long-standing penchant for mechanical correctness. Drawing on such figures as Stuart Hall, Terry Eagleton, Louis Althusser, and Michel Foucault, she explains how composition itself emerged from a dubious institutional agenda. In the late nineteenth century, Miller points out, the American academy sought to incorporate a broader range of students while maintaining old social hierarchies. Composition emerged as the ideal sorting mechanism: certain students would have to undergo its "low" rituals of purification, while others could proceed to the "high" study of literature. Composition, Miller argues, broke from the rhetorical tradition when it constructed the student writer as a particular human subject, one who concentrates on private, individual experience. To reverse this drift, Miller suggests, present-day composition specialists must emphasize the social functions of writing and cultivate the historiography that she has demonstrated.

Kathleen McCormick also refers to theorists associated with British cultural studies as she examines a typical composition assignment, the research paper. McCormick points out that when textbooks discuss this assignment, they often give a conflicting message: even though they indicate that sources are subjective, they press students to be objective in researching and writing papers. McCormick emphasizes that an ideal research paper would not embrace relativism. Rather, she would have students place their perspectives, as well as those of their sources, in a historical context. Students doing this kind of research would probe contradictions among sources, acknowledge marginalized voices, note the effects of various ideological positions, and envision better discursive practices.

A similar concern with society, history, and culture leads James Slevin to challenge the way in which writing courses usually teach classic essays. Centering his discussion on the composition favorite

"Democracy," by E. B. White, he observes that anthologies like *The Norton Reader* (Eastman) and theorists like Frederic Bogel encourage a formalist appreciation of the piece. Slevin would have students use critical theory to examine the essay as a debatable response to exigencies of its time, an approach he demonstrates by looking to the *New Yorker* issue where it first appeared. In addition to reviewing the strategies of White's text, Slevin analyzes other texts in the same issue, showing how they all seek to negotiate relations of gender, race, and class.

Alluding to a wide range of theorists, Kurt Spellmeyer critiques a more recent development in composition: its focus on the conventions of various discourse communities. Above all, he questions Kenneth Bruffee's influential view of how knowledge is socially constructed. In brief, Spellmeyer claims that Bruffee ignores power relations and the ways that people can challenge discursive constraints. While he admits that Bruffee's emphasis on social context is a significant advance over the empiricism of Locke, he believes that Bruffee slights the institutional and political circumstances in which knowledge is produced and circulated. The idea, suggested by the sociologist Max Weber, that modern society is an "iron cage" can help counterbalance Bruffee's idealism. Spellmeyer argues, however, that Weber resembles Bruffee in underestimating people's ability to resist conventions. Elaborating a more optimistic view of human agency, Spellmeyer cites studies of convicts who alter prison policies. He also finds support in the anthropology of Victor Turner and Sally Falk Moore, who depict culture as a dynamic process rather than as a fixed set of rules.

Suzanne Clark expresses another concern about writing theory's turn to social constructionism. Even though she admires much about the development, she fears that it will perpetuate the modern intellectual tradition of denigrating the sentimental. Clark argues that feminists should be especially concerned, because sentimental discourse has usually been linked to women. She finds Julia Kristeva's work helpful in its envisioning of a more central place in academic reason for this discourse and for women themselves. Academic reason's contempt for sentimentality has entailed contempt for rhetoric as well, in particular for the appeals of ethos and pathos. By neglecting these elements of classical rhetoric, Clark asserts, academic reason limits its own public influence. She believes that social-constructionist writing theory will meet the same fate if it insists on excluding the sentimental.

Like Clark, Susan Wells relates contemporary theory to classical thinking, but her essay focuses on what writing teachers might learn from student writing and from three texts: Plato's *Phaedrus*, Jasper